Is the *Reformation* FINISHED?

Tim Rumsey

The author assumes full responsibility for the accuracy of all facts and quotations as cited in this book. The opinions expressed in this book are the author's personal views and interpretations, and do not necessarily reflect those of the publisher.

This book is provided with the understanding that the publisher is not engaged in giving spiritual, legal, medical, or other professional advice. If authoritative advice is needed, the reader should seek the counsel of a competent professional.

ISBN-13: 978-1-4796-0835-5 (Paperback)
ISBN-13: 978-1-4796-0836-2 (ePub)
ISBN-13: 978-1-4796-0837-9 (Mobi)
Library of Congress Control Number: 2017917518

Published by

Table of Contents

Preface

Is the Reformation finished? Was it simply a passing family feud within Christianity, an insignificant historical footnote with little relevance to modern life? This book suggests otherwise, and argues that the primary issue behind the Reformation matters more today than it did 500 years ago. The final battle still lies ahead. The Reformation is not finished; it has only just begun!

About the Author

Tim Rumsey is Speaker/Director of Pathway to Paradise Ministries, and is an associate speaker with White Horse Media. He is the host of "Pictures of the End," a weekly podcast and radio show heard on stations across North America. His passion is to share the Bible's good news for today through the written and spoken word. He lives with his wife, Stacey, and their children in Missouri. For more information about Pathway to Paradise Ministries, visit www.PathwayToParadise.org.

Introduction

On October 31, 1517, a Roman Catholic priest named Martin Luther nailed ninety-five theses, or protests, on the church door in Wittenberg, Germany. The document outlined doctrinal errors and ethical hypocrisies that Luther perceived in the Roman Catholic Church, and it ignited a firestorm of religious controversy throughout Europe. Five hundred years later, numerous influential voices insist that the Reformation is over. Their statements sound like this:

- "Luther's protest is over. Is yours?"[1]
- "We are witnessing the demise of Protestantism."[2]

---

1. Tony Palmer, Address to evangelical leaders, http://1ref.us/ki (accessed August 14, 2017).
2. John Hall, quoted in Jim Ashley, "Death of Protestantism Foreseen," *Chattanooga Free Press*, editor's note (May 10, 1997).

- "We are seeing the ending of Protestantism as it is known and do not know what will follow."[3]
- "I'm eradicating the word 'Protestant' even out of my vocabulary…I'm not protesting anything…it's time for Catholics and non-Catholics to come together as one in the Spirit and one in the Lord."[4]
- "It's time for Protestants to go to the shepherd and say, 'What do we have to do to come home?'"[5]
- "Our Protestant assumptions have been all wrong."[6]

What are—or at least, what were—the Protestant assumptions? Historically they have been summarized as the "five *solas*:" *sola scriptura* (the Bible alone), *sola fide* (by faith alone), *solus Christus* (through Christ alone), *soli Deo gloria* (for God's glory alone), and *sola gratia* (by grace alone). The Protestant reformers taught that salvation is available on an individual basis, independent from the mediation of the Roman Church[7], through faith alone in Jesus Christ. Furthermore, they believed that everything necessary for one

3. Ben Johnson, quoted in Jim Ashley, "Death of Protestantism Foreseen," *Chattanooga Free Press*, editor's note (May 10, 1997).
4. Paul Crouch, "Praise the Lord Program," Trinity Broadcasting Network (October 17, 1989).
5. Robert Schuller, *Calvary Contender* (November 15, 1987).
6. Tom Olden, quoted in Jim Ashley, "Death of Protestantism Foreseen," *Chattanooga Free Press*, editor's note (May 10, 1997).
7. This book refers to the Roman Catholic Church also as "the Church" and the "Roman Church."

to understand and experience salvation is revealed and explained in the Bible. The Roman Catholic Church disagreed, insisting that salvation is available only through the Church, and that Church tradition is as authoritative as Scripture for determining truth.

Today, many are suggesting that the Protestant assumptions have run their course. In 1999 the Lutheran World Federation and the Roman Catholic Church signed a *Joint Declaration on the Doctrine of Justification*, which stated, "this Joint Declaration is able to formulate a consensus on basic truths concerning the doctrine of justification. In light of this consensus, the corresponding doctrinal condemnations of the sixteenth century do not apply to today's partner."[8] Many hailed the agreement as a sign that the centuries-old division between Protestantism and Catholicism is nearly finished.

For instance, in 2010, Eric Bergman, a Catholic priest and former Episcopalian minister, stated, "If we look at histories, heresies run themselves out after about 500 years. I believe we are seeing the last gasp of the Reformation in the mainline Protestant groups."[9] An apparent agreement on the theological definition of justification, however, hardly signals the end of the Reformation. Luther's primary concern when he posted the ninety-five theses was the abuse of indulgences, and as the Reformation progressed the reformers found themselves at odds with Rome on *numerous* issues including papal authority, the legitimacy of tradition as a source of theological

8. http://1ref.us/kk (accessed August 14, 2017).
9. http://1ref.us/kl (accessed August 14, 2017).

truth, transubstantiation, the Immaculate Conception and exaltation of Mary, the veneration of saints, the role and function of the human priesthood, and the bulwark of sacerdotalism, on which the Roman Catholic Church is built.

Notwithstanding these numerous doctrinal differences, all of which still exist between Roman Catholicism and biblical Christianity, recent ecumenical events have accelerated the push to declare the Reformation finished. In 2014, Tony Palmer, an Episcopalian bishop and personal friend of Pope Francis, addressed a gathering of evangelical leaders. Referring to the Joint Declaration signed in 1999 between Lutherans and Catholics, Palmer said, "Luther's protest is over. Is yours?"[10] He then shared an iPhone recording of Pope Francis inviting evangelicals to "come home" to the Roman Catholic Church. The crowd's response was enthusiastic, and several months later Palmer led a group of evangelical leaders to an unprecedented meeting with Pope Francis at the Vatican.

The year 2016 brought an acceleration of ecumenical activities aimed at healing the wounds between Rome and Protestantism. In June of 2016, Pope Francis became the first pope to visit a Waldensian church. The Waldensian movement, an early precursor to the Protestant Reformation, was branded as heretical in the Middle Ages and Pope Innocent VIII ordered its extermination in 1487. Pope Francis apologized for this persecution, and then appealed for unity: "On

10. http://1ref.us/km (accessed August 14, 2017).

behalf of the Catholic Church, I ask forgiveness for the un-Christian and even inhumane positions and actions taken against you historically. In the name of the Lord Jesus Christ, forgive us!"[11]

Later in 2016, Pope Francis visited Malmo, Sweden, to observe the 499th anniversary of Luther's protest. A joint declaration issued by the Pope and Lutheran leaders stated, "We long for this wound in the body of Christ to be healed. This is the goal of our ecumenical endeavors."[12] One year later, on October 31, 2017, the Lutheran World Federation and the Pontifical Council for Promoting Christian Unity issued a joint statement that read in part, "We recognize that while the past cannot be changed, its influence upon us today can be transformed to become a stimulus for growing communion, and a sign of hope for the world to overcome division and fragmentation. Again, it has become clear that what we have in common is far more than that which still divides us."[13]

Is the Reformation finished? Was it simply a passing family feud, an insignificant historical footnote with little relevance to modern life? This book suggests otherwise, and argues that the primary issue behind the Reformation matters more today than it did 500 years ago.

---

11. http://1ref.us/kn (accessed August 14, 2017).
12. http://1ref.us/ko (accessed August 14, 2017).
13. "Joint Statement by the Lutheran World Federation and the Pontifical Council for Promoting Christian Unity on the conclusion of the year of the common commemoration of the Reformation, 31st October 2017"; accessed November 1, 2017; http://press.vatican.va/content/salastampa/en/bollettino/pubblico/2017/10/31/171031a.html

The Keys of Heaven

"In the Reformation the principle issue at stake was one of authority."[14]
Harry Lee Poe and Jimmy H. Davis

When Martin Luther posted his ninety-five theses, he was a devoted servant of the church he loved. A Catholic monk and theologian, his aim was to reform abuses he perceived in the church—not to splinter Christianity. The nails that sunk into the church door, however, quickly fractured a religious and political system that had dominated Europe for 1,000 years. The Roman Catholic Church controlled life in medieval Europe. Its laws governed most aspects of religious and civil life, including marriage, wills, and what we would today call

---

14. Harry Lee Poe and Jimmy H. Davis, *God and the Cosmos: Divine Activity in Space, Time and History* (Downers Grove, Illinois: InterVarsity Press, 2012), p. 60.

"moral legislation"—laws concerning things such as adultery, fornication, and blasphemy.

The nails that sunk into the church door … quickly fractured a religious and political system that had dominated Europe for 1,000 years.

> [T]here was no distinction between church and state, or even between church and community: to be a part of society was to be part of the church… The church had its own law code, called canon law, and a system of church courts to enforce it, exercising authority over many aspects of people's lives.[15]

The pope controlled affairs both inside and outside the church, and his power and influence frequently exceeded that of most political leaders today. "The pope as vicar of Christ claimed headship over the entire Church on earth, *with supreme authority in the Church and also over the nations*, with right to set up and depose princes and monarchs."[16] Augustine, the Church father often regarded as the founder of medieval Catholic theology, argued that Rome had always been supreme over the churches. His classic book, *The City of God,* presented the Catholic ideal of a universal church in control of a universal state, and his vision provided the theoretical basis for the medieval papacy. Throughout the middle ages the Church asserted its absolute spiritual and civil authority, even

15. Jeffrey L. Singman, *Daily Life in Medieval Europe* (Westport, Connecticut: Greenwood Press, 1999), p. 12.
16. Presbyterian Church in the U.S.A., *The Protestant Reformation and Its Influence, 1517-1917* (BiblioLife, 2015), p. 9, emphasis added.

though in actual practice it was not always able to exercise those claims.

Central to the pope's claim to authority was a statement that Jesus Christ once made to His disciple Peter:

> And I also say to you that you are Peter, and on this rock I will build My church, and the gates of Hades shall not prevail against it. And I will give you the keys of the kingdom of heaven, and whatever you bind on earth will be bound in heaven, and whatever you loose on earth will be loosed in heaven (Matthew 16:18–19).

The Church interpreted this verse to mean that Jesus Christ designated the disciple Peter as the foundation and head of the Christian church. Peter's authority, in turn, presumably passed in an unbroken line through successive Roman bishops and popes. This doctrine of apostolic succession became fully crystallized under Pope Leo I in the fifth century.

> Leo I (the Great, d. 461) was the first bishop of Rome to proclaim that Peter had been the first pope, to assert the succession of the papacy from Peter, to claim primacy directly from Jesus Christ, and to succeed in applying these principles to papal administration of the affairs of the church. Leo I gave to the theory of papal power its final form, and made that power a reality.[17]

17. Francis D. Nichol, ed., "Additional Note on Chapter 7," *Seventh-day Adventist Bible Commentary*, vol. 4 (Washington, DC: Review and Herald Publishing Association, 1955), p. 836.

Leo's claims became fundamental to the medieval Church's self-understanding, and they remain so today for the contemporary Catholic Church. The *Catholic Encyclopedia* states that "the Roman Pontiffs come immediately after, occupy the position, and perform the functions of St. Peter; they are, therefore, his successors."[18]

The Protestant reformers were not convinced. If Jesus had invested Peter with absolute power and authority over the church, why had it taken over 400 years for the leader of that church to recognize and claim this authority? In reality, the historical and Biblical evidence suggests that the other disciples and the earliest Christians never viewed Peter this way. Even after Jesus made this statement to Peter, the disciples continued to argue who among them was the greatest (see Luke 22:24; Matthew 18:1; Mark 9:33–35), a strange habit if Jesus had indeed designated Peter as chief of the disciples. Furthermore, in the establishment of the early church, it was James, not Peter, who often appeared in leadership roles. When the church met at a council to consider the question of circumcision for Gentiles, Peter gave his testimony of how God had shown him that the Gentiles could share in the gospel (Acts 15:6–11). It was James, however, who issued the last word, saying, "Therefore I judge that we should not trouble those from among the Gentiles who are turning to God, but that we write to them to abstain from things polluted by idols, from sexual

18. Joseph Wilhelm, "Apostolic Succession," *The Catholic Encyclopedia*, vol. 1 (New York: Robert Appleton Company, 1907), http://1ref.us/kq (accessed August 14, 2017).

immorality, from things strangled, and from blood" (Acts 15:19–20).

Questions also arose regarding Paul's actions toward Peter. After his conversion to Christ, Paul approached "James, Cephas [Peter], and John, who seemed to be pillars" (Galatians 2:9), and requested that they extend the "right hand of fellowship" to him as a fellow apostle. If Jesus had clearly established Peter as the head of the church, why did Paul list James and John as pillars of the church along with Peter? Some time later, after Peter had refused to eat with some Gentiles because of the presence of other Jews, Paul "withstood [Peter] to his face, because he was to be blamed" (Galatians 2:11). Again, if Peter held absolute authority in the church, why did Paul confront him in this way? Furthermore, the Biblical evidence suggests that Peter considered Jesus the true Rock and foundation of the church. Speaking before the Jewish council, Peter referred to Jesus as "the stone which was rejected by you builders, which has become the chief cornerstone" (Acts 4:11).

In reality, the pope claims the authority, not of Peter, but of Jesus Christ. The Bible identifies two primary aspects of Christ's authority—His *teaching authority* and His *governing authority*. Matthew 7:29 says that Jesus "taught them as one having authority, and not as the scribes." In another passage, Jesus referred to His governing authority by saying, "All authority has been given to Me in heaven and on earth" (Matthew 28:18). According to the Church, the pope's authority is also two-fold, and it imitates the authority of Jesus Christ. The Church's "official teaching has made clear that the pope possesses (a) an *infallible teaching authority* whose exercise leads to doctrines that are irreformable without the consent of the Church, and (b) an *ultimate governing authority* which is supreme, [and] universal."[19]

In other words, the pope can define doctrine *ex cathedra* (literally "from the chair," or by virtue of his teaching authority), and he can enforce that teaching with his absolute governing authority. When Pope Leo XIII clarified the Roman Church's teaching on papal authority, the pope's authority was equated with God's authority. "But the supreme teacher in the Church is the Roman Pontiff. Union of minds, therefore, requires, together with a perfect accord in the one faith, complete submission and obedience of will to the Church and to the Roman Pontiff, *as to God Himself*."[20] Additionally, the pope claims "ultimate governing authority," a power that was clarified in the 1960s during the Second Vatican Council: "[T]he Roman Pontiff...the successor of Peter, the Vicar of Christ, the visible Head of the whole Church, govern[s] the house of the living God."[21]

The Protestant reformers believed the papal claims of authority to be blasphemous, and responded by labeling the pope as the dreaded antichrist of Bible prophecy. The issue of authority quickly became the primary

---

19. Gary Chamberlain and Patrick J. Howell, *Empowering Authority: The Charisms of Episcopacy and Primacy in the Church* (Kansas City: Sheed & Ward, 1990), p. 48, emphasis added.
20. Pope Leo XIII, "On the Chief Duties of Christians as Citizens," January 10, 1890, trans. in *The Great Encyclical Letters of Pope Leo XIII* (New York: Benziger, 1903), p. 193, emphasis added.
21. Pope Paul VI, *Lumen Gentium*, par. 18 (November 21, 1964), http://1ref.us/kr (accessed August 14, 2017).

catalyst in the conflict between Protestants and Rome, and the Reformation's two major battlegrounds—the authority of the Bible and the doctrine of justification—were really debates on the legitimacy of papal authority.

One important key to the papacy's presumed authority lay in its control of Scripture. Before the invention of the printing press, copies of the Bible were scarce, and the Church carefully guarded the few Latin copies that existed. This inaccessibility of the Bible to the vast majority of Christians during the Middle Ages contributed greatly to the effectiveness of the pope's authoritative claims.

> The Bible would exalt God and place finite men in their true position...For hundreds of years the circulation of the Bible was prohibited. The people were forbidden to read it or to have it in their houses, and unprincipled priests and prelates interpreted its teachings to sustain their pretensions. Thus the pope came to be almost universally acknowledged as the vicegerent of God on earth, endowed with authority over church and state.[22]

Two centuries before Luther's iconic stand, John Wycliffe translated the Bible from Latin into English, and laid a foundation for the work of later reformers. Vernacular translations of the Bible reproduced on the printing press in the middle of the fifteenth century opened the way for the Reformation's explosive growth in the sixteenth century. Efforts at reform had occurred before Luther, but never before had the

22. Ellen G. White, *The Great Controversy* (Boise, ID: Pacific Press Publishing Association, 1911), p. 51.

common people been able to read the Bible in their own language.

It is not surprising, therefore, that the authority of the Bible was the Reformation's first big battleground issue. The question was simple: Is the Bible, or the Church and its traditions, the Christian's ultimate authority? The *Catholic Encyclopedia* outlines the two positions:

... never before had the common people been able to read the Bible in their own language.

> The Protestant principle is: The Bible and nothing but the Bible; the Bible, according to them, is the sole theological source; there are no revealed truths save the truths contained in the Bible; according to them the Bible is the sole rule of faith: by it and by it alone should all dogmatic questions be solved; it is the only binding *authority*. Catholics, on the other hand, hold that...Holy Scripture is...not the only theological source of the Revelation made by God to His Church. Side by side with Scripture there is tradition, side by side with the written revelation there is the oral revelation. This granted, *it is impossible to be satisfied with the Bible alone for the solution of all dogmatic questions. Such was the first field of controversy between Catholic theologians and the Reformers.*[23]

The Protestants upheld the Bible as an unchanging, authoritative expression of truth and God's will.

---

23. Jean Bainvel, "Tradition and Living Magisterium," *The Catholic Encyclopedia*, vol. 15 (New York: Robert Appleton Company, 1912), http://1ref.us/ks (accessed August 14, 2017).

How could tradition, which was passed on orally in Christianity's early centuries and only later written down, prove to be a reliable guide to truth? How could one know which traditions are of divine origin and which are purely human? The Catholic answer, again, was found in Church authority, and is reflected in a recent article on Catholic.org: "How can we know which traditions are apostolic and which are merely human? The answer is the same as how we know which scriptures are apostolic and which are merely human—*by listening to the magisterium or teaching authority of Christ's Church*."[24]

John Calvin, founder of the Presbyterian Church, recognized that the debate about the authority of the Bible was really a contest on papal authority. "[T]he difference between us and the papists," he wrote,

> is that they believe that the church cannot be the pillar of the truth unless she presides over the Word of God. We, on the other hand, assert that it is because she reverently subjects herself to the Word of God that the truth is preserved by her, and passed on to others by her hands.[25]

Like Calvin, Luther argued that the Church's authority was subservient to the authority of the Bible, not the other way around. "[Luther] firmly declared that Christians should receive no other doctrines than

---

24. "Scripture and Tradition," http://1ref.us/kt (accessed August 14, 2017).
25. Alister E. McGrath, *Reformation Thought, An Introduction*, 2d ed. (Oxford: Wiley, 1993), p. 143, quoted in Helen Parish, Elaine Fulton, and Peter Webster, eds., *The Search for Authority in Reformation Europe* (Farnham: Ashgate Publishing Ltd., 2014), p. 4.

those which rest on the *authority* of the Sacred Scriptures. These words struck at the very foundation of papal supremacy. *They contained the vital principle of the Reformation.*"[26] The question on the authority of the Bible, however, was not the only divisive issue in Reformation. Equally fundamental to the Protestant mindset was its rebuttal of papal claims to authority in and over the process of justification. We will turn to this debate in the next chapter.

26. Ellen G. White, *The Great Controversy* (Boise, ID: Pacific Press Publishing Association, 1911), p. 125, emphasis added.

Justification, Authority, and the Priesthood

"When the article of justification has fallen, everything has fallen."[27] Martin Luther

The question of authority also spilled over into the debate on justification, the Reformation's second big battleground issue. Justification is a legal term—think of it as the opposite of condemnation. Today we might compare justification to being acquitted of a crime. When a person is justified, God no longer considers them guilty for the sins they have committed, for "the judgment *which came* from one *offense resulted* in condemnation, but the free gift *which came* from many offenses *resulted* in justification" (Romans 5:16). On this point Catholics and Protestants agree. What has separated them for half a millennium is the

27. Edwald M. Plass, ed., *What Luther Says: an anthology,* vol. 2 (Concordia Publishing House, 1959), p. 715.

explanation of *how* justification is accomplished in a person's life.

The biblical doctrine of justification is inseparably linked to the authority and priesthood of Jesus Christ. Shortly before He ascended to heaven, Jesus told His disciples, "All authority is given to Me in heaven and on earth" (Matthew 28:18). The book of Hebrews explains what Jesus did with this authority after His ascension to heaven—He became humanity's High Priest. "Seeing then that we have a great High Priest who has passed through the heavens, Jesus the Son of God, let us hold fast our confession" (Hebrews 4:14). The Bible even identifies *where* in heaven Jesus serves as High Priest—in the heavenly sanctuary. "We have such a High Priest, who is seated at the right hand of the throne of the Majesty in the heavens; a Minister of the sanctuary and of the true tabernacle which the Lord erected, and not man" (Hebrews 8:1–2).

In the Old Testament sacrificial services, a priest was required to make the animal sacrifices valid, for only priests were allowed to carry the blood into the holy places of the tabernacle as an atonement for sin. Without a priest, forgiveness was impossible and the guilt of sin remained. The entire system of animal sacrifices and human priests, however, was in itself of absolutely no value to save, for they "cannot make him who performed the service perfect" (Hebrews 9:9). Instead, their purpose was to point forward to Jesus Christ.

Just like the Old Testament earthly priests carried the sacrificial blood into the earthly sanctuary, Jesus entered heaven's sanctuary as humanity's High Priest through the merits of His blood. Hebrews 9:12

says, "Not with the blood of goats and calves, but with His own blood He entered the Most Holy Place once for all, having obtained eternal redemption." When a person repents of sin, they are "justified by His blood" (Romans 5:9), but that justification doesn't stop with forgiveness. Christ's role as High Priest gives Him the authority to apply the righteous merits of His blood to the lives of repentant sinners, so that they now have His power to overcome temptation and sin. "How much more shall the blood of Christ, who through the eternal Spirit offered Himself without spot to God, cleanse your conscience from dead works to serve the living God" (Hebrews 9:14)? This is the end result of justification—a legal declaration of forgiveness backed up by a transformed life.

The Bible teaches that salvation comes only through Jesus Christ and His priestly ministration. "Neither is there salvation in any other, for there is no other name under heaven given among men by which we must be saved" (Acts 4:12). Justification comes through the authority of Christ's priesthood, and is available to all people individually through faith in Christ. This is the basic doctrine of justification taught by Luther and the other reformers. In *On the Papacy in Rome*, Luther wrote, "Christ is a spiritual, internal priest; for he is seated in heaven and intercedes for us as a priest; he teaches internally, in the heart, and does what a priest is supposed to do between God and us."[28]

---

28. J. Pelikan and H.T. Lehmann, eds., *Luther's Works,* vol. 39 (St. Louis and Philadelphia: Concordia Publishing House/Muhlenberg Press, 1958–67), p. 80, quoted in Gerald O'Collins and Michael Keenan Jones, *Jesus Our Priest: A Christian Approach to the Priesthood of Christ* (Oxford: Oxford University Press, 2010), pp. 128–129.

In Roman Catholic doctrine, justification likewise rests on the authority of the priesthood, but, in practicality, it is a human priesthood with the pope as its head. In the Catholic system justification is sacerdotal—it requires the ministration of priests who administer sacraments, which are "external, visible ceremonies…by which certain graces [are] conferred on men."[29] At the council of Trent, it was confirmed that the "sacraments have then first the power of sanctifying when one uses them."[30] Participation in the sacraments is essential; in the words of Pope Francis, God "gives us salvation through the sacraments."[31]

In the Roman Catholic system, therefore, justification is available only through the authority of the Church, because only the pope and priests can administer the sacraments, which are essential to salvation.

> The priesthood claimed the right of deciding the eternal destiny of every mortal man. This right was exercised through the sacraments, declared to be the necessary channels of grace and eternal life. *Apart from these sacraments, it was taught, there can be no forgiveness of sins and no entrance into the fellowship of Christ; the priest alone has authority to administer them*; moreover, his administration invariably makes them efficient.[32]

---

29. Daniel Kennedy, "Sacraments," *The Catholic Encyclopedia,* vol. 13 (New York: Robert Appleton Company, 1912), http://1ref.us/ku (accessed August 14, 2017).
30. *The canons and decrees of the sacred and oecumenical Council of Trent*, ed. and trans. by J. Waterworth (London: Dolman, 1848), p. 77, http://1ref.us/kv (accessed August 14, 2017).
31. Pope Francis, online video, http://1ref.us/kw (accessed August 14, 2017).
32. Church in the U.S.A., *The Protestant Reformation and Its Influence, 1517–1917* (BiblioLife, 2015), pp. 9–10, emphasis added.

In the Roman Catholic system, therefore, justification is available only through the authority of the Church, because only the pope and priests can administer the sacraments, which are essential to salvation.

Taking the Catholic doctrine of justification to its logical end, Pope Boniface VIII in 1302 declared, "Furthermore, we declare, we proclaim, we define that it is absolutely necessary for salvation that every human creature be subject to the Roman Pontiff."[33] In the Roman Catholic system, justification and human salvation had *everything* to do with Church authority.

Here's how it worked. Medieval Europe was feudalistic—each level of society was controlled and protected by the level above. Absolute fealty and obedience to one's lord, or master, were expected. The bonds between a vassal, or servant, and his or her lord were permanent and inflexible, and the *authority* of lord over vassal was absolute. For a vassal to disobey his or her lord was considered a felony,[34] and the resulting societal structure resembled "an inter-connected pyramid that…culminated in the apex of the king."[35]

The Roman Catholic Church in the middle ages was structured much like the feudal system. When someone entered the church through baptism they were considered to have placed themselves under

---

33. Pope Boniface VIII, *Unam Sanctum* (1302), http://1ref.us/kx (accessed August 14, 2017).
34. Bede Jarret, "Feudalism," *The Catholic Encyclopedia*, vol. 6 (New York: Robert Appleton Company, 1909), http://1ref.us/ky (accessed August 14, 2017).
35. Ibid.

the authority of the church. "[T]he *baptizatus* [person baptized] was freed from the burdens of sin but held by an obligation to submit to ecclesiastical *authority*."[36] In return for the promise of justification, salvation, and eternal life, the baptized church member swore obedience to the church.

> The *fides* [loyalty] which the individual promised the Church in baptism now resembled the objective legal obligation which arose from a contract, isolated from the psychological complexities of the theological concepts of faith and belief. The fundamental metaphor of *sacramentum* [sacraments] as contract gave rise to a series of others in which the faith of the individual was adjudicated as the terms of a contract would be in the eyes of the law.[37]

In other words, the terms of the "baptismal contract" were expressed in the sacraments, and when someone sinned and broke their "contract" of loyalty to the church, forgiveness and justification were available through the sacrament of penance, which could be administered only through a priest's authority.

The sacrament of penance, or confession, "assume[d] the character of a legal trial, with accusation, sentence and satisfaction."[38] The absolution, or forgiveness, from sin that was the end goal of penance

---

36. Brian Tierney and Peter Linehan, *Authority and Power: Studies on Medieval Law and Government Presented to Walter Ullmann on his seventieth birthday* (Cambridge: Cambridge University Press, 1980), p. 92, emphasis added.
37. Ibid, p. 97.
38. "Sacrament of Penance," Catholic Online, http://1ref.us/kz (accessed August 14, 2017).

was available only through the authority of the priest as a "keeper of the keys." The Church taught that

> Christ gave *authority*, the keys, to the apostles to forgive sin, to decide between absolving or retaining guilt. This requires 'confession' of sins for this judgment not to be arbitrary, hence the popular name of the sacrament. *This authority was passed on to bishops, and from them to priests, with ordination.*[39]

The priest's decision as to whether forgiveness should be granted was final, which meant that his control over the eternal destiny of the sinner was absolute. One of the more extreme statements of papal authority in this regard was penned in 1483, just 34 years before Luther nailed his ninety-five theses to the church door.

> [N]o appeal holds when made from the Pope to God, because there is one consistory of the Pope himself and of God Himself, of which consistory the Pope himself is the key-bearer and the doorkeeper. Therefore no one can appeal from the Pope to God, as no one can enter into the consistory of God without the mediation of the Pope, who is the key-bearer and the doorkeeper of the consistory of eternal life; and as no one can appeal to himself, because there is one decision and one court curia of God and of the Pope.[40]

---

39. Colin B. Donovan, "Sacraments in Scripture," http://1ref.us/10 (accessed August 14, 2017), emphasis added.
40. Augustinus Triumphus, "De Papalis Sentencie Apellatione," *Summa de Potestate Ecclesiastica,* fol. 61 v (Augustae Vindelicorum Augsburg, 1483), question 6.

Not only was the priest's decision to forgive sins absolute, so was his power to dictate the punishment that the repentant sinner must perform in order to satisfy the demands of justice. This punishment was commonly referred to as "satisfaction." Because of the legal nature of the "contract" between the Church and its members, the priest's decision was binding. For medieval Christians living under Church control, justification had less to do with faith in the blood of Jesus than it did obedience to the authority of priests, bishops, and popes.

It remains the same today. The current Catholic Catechism states,

> Beneath the changes in discipline and celebration that [penance] has undergone over the centuries, the same fundamental structure is to be discerned...the bishop and his priests forgives sins in the name of Jesus Christ and determines the manner of satisfaction.[41]

According to the *Catholic Encyclopedia*, "The quality and extent of the penance is determined by the confessor [priest]," and the repentant person is "under obligation to continue the performance of his penance until it is completed."[42]

Justification in the Roman Catholic system remains inseparable from the authority of the human priesthood. Christ's authority as High Priest in heaven's temple has been substituted for human authority.

---

41. *Catechism of the Catholic Church*, par. 1448, http://1ref.us/l1 (accessed August 14, 2017).
42. Edward Hanna, "The Sacrament of Penance," *The Catholic Encyclopedia*, vol. 11 (New York: Robert Appleton Company, 1911), http://1ref.us/l2 (accessed August 14, 2017).

William Webster, a former Roman Catholic, sums up the issue this way:

> Roman Catholic teaching in its exaltation of tradition, the papacy, and the church is a depreciation of the authority of Scripture and the supreme authority of Jesus Christ. In the end, the Roman church has displaced divine authority with human authority.[43]

Virtually every Roman Catholic doctrine challenged or rejected by the Protestants had its foundation, at some level, in papal authority. Take transubstantiation, for instance. Transubstantiation is the teaching that the bread and wine offered in the sacrament of the Eucharist literally become the body and blood of Jesus Christ. It was declared as dogma at the Fourth Lateran Council in 1215, and according to the current Catechism of the Catholic Church,

Virtually every Roman Catholic doctrine challenged or rejected by the Protestants had its foundation, at some level, in papal authority.

> By the consecration the transubstantiation of the bread and wine into the Body and Blood of Christ is brought about. Under the consecrated species of bread and wine Christ himself, living and glorious, is present in a true, real, and substantial manner: his Body and his Blood, with his soul and his divinity.[44]

---

43. William Webster, "Did I Really Leave the Holy Catholic Church?" in *Roman Catholicism*, John Armstrong, ed. (Chicago: Moody Press, 1994), p. 285.
44. *Catechism of the Catholic Church*, par. 1413, http://1ref.us/l3 (accessed August 14, 2017).

The heart of the Roman Catholic mass is transubstantiation, or the "most holy Eucharist," in which it is taught that "the Author Himself of sanctity" is literally present.[45] According to Roman doctrine, the priest's authoritative command transforms the bread and wine into the literal body and blood of Jesus Christ:

> The supreme power of the priestly office is the power of consecrating [transubstantiation]...In this essential phase of the sacred ministry, the power of the priest is not surpassed by that of the bishop, the archbishop, the cardinal or the pope. Indeed it is equal to that of Jesus Christ. *For in this role the priest speaks with the voice and the authority of God Himself*...[T]he priest brings Christ down from heaven, and renders Him present on our altar as the eternal Victim for the sins of man—not once but a thousand times! The priest speaks and lo! Christ, the eternal and omnipotent God, bows his head in humble obedience to the priest's command.[46]

The reformers opposed the idea that any human priest has this kind of authority. In 1563, the Church of England stated in its *Thirty-Nine Articles*:

> Transubstantiation (or the change of the substance of bread and wine) in the Supper of the Lord, cannot be proved by Holy Writ; but is repugnant to the plain words of Scripture, overthroweth the

---

45. *The canons and decrees of the sacred and oecumenical Council of Trent*, ed. and trans. J. Waterworth (London: Dolman, 1848), pp. 77–78, http://1ref.us/kv (accessed August 14, 2017).
46. John O'Brien, *The Faith of Millions* (Huntington, IN: Our Sunday Visitor, Inc., 1974), pp. 255–256, emphasis added.

nature of a Sacrament, and hath given occasion to many superstitions.[47]

Luther was more blunt and wrote, "the Church had the true faith for more than twelve hundred years, during which time the holy Fathers never once mentioned this transubstantiation—certainly, a monstrous word for a monstrous idea."[48]

Rome's claims to authority were also reflected in its teachings about Mary, the saints, and the "treasury of merit" that purportedly flows from their good works. The Church claims, through the "power of the keys," to be in control of a "vast and inexhaustible treasury...[that] may be drawn upon in payment of temporal punishment."[49] While the merits of Christ's sacrifice form the principle fund of this treasury, "this treasury includes as well the prayers and good works of the Blessed Virgin Mary...In the treasury, too, are the prayers and good works of all the saints."[50] The Church is in charge of this "treasury of merit," and can make it available to people as determined by its authority. The Catholic priest John O'Brien stated, "It is part of the authority committed by Christ to Peter and his successors to specify to what extent, and under what conditions, the funds of this common treasury

---

47. "Article 28," *The Thirty-nine Articles of the Church of England Explained*, 6th ed. (Methuen & Company, 1908), p. 640.
48. Martin Luther, *The Babylonian Captivity of the Church*, http://1ref.us/l4 (accessed August 14, 2017).
49. John O'Brien, *The Faith of Millions* (Huntington, IN: Our Sunday Visitor, Inc., 1974), p. 198.
50. *Catechism of the Catholic Church*, par. 1476, http://1ref.us/l5 (accessed August 14, 2017).

shall be made available to the individual members."[51]

Indulgences, which distribute the "treasury of merit" to individuals, grant people "the remission of the temporal punishments due for their sins."[52] Indulgences are distributed by the Church "by virtue of the power of binding and loosing granted her by Christ Jesus."[53] The *Code of Canon Law* stipulates that the pope, as a "minister of redemption[,] dispenses and applies *authoritatively* the treasury of the satisfactions of Christ and the saints."[54] O'Brien underscores this in his book *The Faith of Millions*: "The authority to grant indulgences, as has been indicated, flows from the power of the keys, the unlimited power of binding and of loosing, conferred by Christ upon St. Peter and his successors."[55]

When Luther posted his ninety-five theses, his primary contention with the church—at that moment, at least—was not Mary, the saints, transubstantiation, justification, nor even the role of Scripture and tradition. His focus was the use, or at least *abuse*, of indulgences. In 1517, the Vatican was in desperate need of finances for the construction of St. Peter's Basilica in Rome. The pope had commissioned Johan Tetzel, a Catholic friar, to raise funds for the massive building project. Tetzel's technique? Sell indulgences.

---

51. John O'Brien, *The Faith of Millions* (Huntington, IN: Our Sunday Visitor, Inc., 1974), p. 199.
52. *Catechism of the Catholic Church*, par. 1478, http://1ref.us/l5 (accessed August 14, 2017).
53. Ibid.
54. *Code of Canon Law*, par. 992, http://1ref.us/l6 (accessed August 14, 2017), emphasis added.
55. John O'Brien, *The Faith of Millions* (Huntington, IN: Our Sunday Visitor, Inc., 1974), p. 199.

> As Tetzel entered a town, a messenger went before him, announcing: "The grace of God and of the holy father is at your gates." ...And the people welcomed the blasphemous pretender as if he were God Himself come down from heaven to them. The infamous traffic was set up in the church, and Tetzel, ascending the pulpit, extolled the indulgences as the most precious gift of God. He declared that by virtue of his certificates of pardon all the sins which the purchaser should afterward desire to commit would be forgiven him, and that "not even repentance is necessary." ...More than this, he assured his hearers that the indulgences had power to save not only the living but the dead; that the very moment the money should clink against the bottom of his chest, the soul in whose behalf it had been paid would escape from purgatory and make its way to heaven.[56]

Luther was incensed by Tetzel's "hard sell," and posted his ninety-five theses as an invitation to anyone that wished to debate him on the subject. In doing so, however, Luther

> not only criticized indulgences as being scandalous, superficial, and harmful but also *dared to make a fundamental attack on the church's reigning structures of authority*. He made the connection between the church's penitential requirements and God's punishment of sin to be the overarching

---

56. Ellen G. White, *The Great Controversy* (Boise, ID: Pacific Press Publishing Association, 1911), p. 127.

> principle of his disputation, in the course of which he denied the pope's authority to bind and loose sins in the hereafter. Luther leveled the authority and efficacy of the papacy, along with all the hierarchical channels underneath it. According to Luther, papal and ecclesiastical sanctions should only apply to this world of the living and not extend somehow beyond death into an ominous purgatory. They have no valid relationship to the transcendent. The pope can therefore release people only from the earthly punishments he himself imposes, not from the punishments that God imposes. *God's judgment is thereby removed in principle from papal authority.*[57]

Luther's attack on papal indulgences had opened a hornet's nest. Rather than invite debate on a single doctrine, the ninety-five theses struck at the heart of papal authority. Though Luther most certainly did not realize in 1517 where this path would lead, the foundation of Roman Christianity had nonetheless been shaken. The basic understanding of how salvation works was suddenly up for grabs, and like the silken strands of a spider's web, every debate, argument, and

Luther's attack on papal indulgences had opened a hornet's nest. Rather than invite debate on a single doctrine, the ninety-five theses struck at the heart of papal authority.

57. Berndt Hamm, *The Early Luther: Stages in a Reformation Reorientation* (Grand Rapids, MI: William B. Eerdmans Publishing Company, 2010), pp. 86–87, emphasis added.

battle that ensued eventually sent aftershocks back to the epicenter of papal authority.

Metal Men and Flying Lions

"He who fears history owns himself conquered."
Anonymous

In many ways, the Protestant Reformation was unintended. John Wycliffe, Jan Hus, John Calvin, Martin Luther, and countless other reformers were all Roman Catholics who desired to reform the Church. As it became clear, however, that the Church, as a whole, was not going to change, the reformers began looking in Scripture for an explanation as to why the "Bride of Christ,"[58] as the Church refers to itself, refused to return to the simplicity and purity of the Biblical gospel. What they discovered shocked them.

Five hundred years before Jesus Christ was born, two men living in ancient Babylon received dreams—

58. *Catechism of the Catholic Church*, par. 808, http://1ref.us/17 (accessed August 14, 2017).

prophetic messages from God. The first was King Nebuchadnezzar. In his dream, he saw a giant statue with a head of gold, chest and arms of silver, belly and thighs of brass, legs of iron, and feet of iron and clay. In the dream, a stone flying in from heaven struck the statue and completely destroyed it. The stone then grew into a mountain that filled the entire earth (Daniel 2:31–35). In the morning, the king knew he had dreamed something important, but couldn't recall the details of the dream. Nebuchadnezzar could find only one man in all of Babylon able to relate and interpret his dream—a Hebrew captive named Daniel.

The next night God revealed to Daniel that Nebuchadnezzar's dream was a prophecy of Earth's future from the time of Babylon until the second coming of Jesus Christ. "Thou art this head of gold" (Daniel 2:38), Daniel told the king, "And after thee shall arise another kingdom, inferior to thee, and another third kingdom of brass" (verse 39). The fourth kingdom, which would be "strong as iron" (verse 40), would eventually fragment into ten parts, represented by the ten toes. The stone, in turn, represented Jesus Christ and the coming kingdom of God. "And in the days of these kings [the ten toes] the God of heaven will set up a kingdom which shall never be destroyed" (verse 44).

Some time later, Daniel himself received a prophetic vision from God. Like Nebuchadnezzar's dream, Daniel's vision predicted the rise and fall of world empires from his day until the second coming of Jesus Christ. Instead of the four metals in Nebuchadnezzar's dream, however, Daniel saw four animals rising from the sea—a lion, a bear, a leopard, and a strange and terrifying beast with iron teeth and ten horns (Daniel 7:3–7). An angel explained to Daniel that the animals represented the progression of world empires, just like in Nebuchadnezzar's dream. "Those great beasts, which are four, are four kings which arise out of the earth" (verse 17). The beasts pointed not to specific kings, but to the kingdoms, or empires, that they represented. "The fourth beast shall be A fourth kingdom on earth, Which shall be different from all other kingdoms" (verse 23). Daniel had been given the same information as King Nebuchadnezzar, only with different symbols!

The two visions identified four sequential empires between Daniel's day and Jesus Christ's second coming. The first empire was Babylon—Daniel had made this clear when he told Nebuchadnezzar, "You are this head of gold." The second and third empires were identified by name in yet another vision recorded in Daniel 8. In this third dream a ram and a goat replaced the beasts of prey in Daniel 7, but the sequence of world empires remained the same. The angel Gabriel told Daniel, "The ram which you saw, having two horns—they are the kings of Media and Persia. And the male goat is the kingdom of Greece" (Daniel 8:20–21).

History reveals the amazing accuracy of Daniel's prophecies. Babylon fell to the Medo-Persian empire in 538 BC when Cyrus' army drained the Euphrates River and marched under the gates of Babylon. Persia, in turn, fell to Alexander the Great and the Greek empire at the battle of Arbela in 331 BC, and Greece fell to the growing Roman Empire in 168 BC at the battle of Pydna. The historian, Paul K. Davis, writes of this battle, "Pydna marked the final destruction of Alexander's empire and introduced Roman authority over the Near East."[59]

Christians have understood this historical fulfillment of Daniel's prophecies for hundreds, even thousands, of years, and it has been the unanimous consent of countless Bible scholars that the fourth empire of Daniel 2 and 7 represents Rome. Hippolytus, who was born less than a hundred years after the disciple John died, wrote about Daniel's prophecies:

> The golden head of the image and the lioness denoted the Babylonians; the shoulders and arms of silver, and the bear, represented the Persians and Medes; the belly and thighs of brass, and the leopard, meant the Greeks, who held the sovereignty from Alexander's time; the legs of iron, and the beast dreadful and terrible, expressed the Romans, who hold the sovereignty at present.[60]

Martin Luther also recognized this prophetic sequence, and identified the fourth beast with iron teeth as the Roman Empire. He wrote, "We must not hold and understand allegories as they sound; as what Daniel says, concerning the beast with ten horns; this we must understand to be spoken of the Roman empire."[61]

---

59. Paul K. Davis, *100 Decisive Battles from Ancient Times to the Present: The World's Major Battles and How They Shaped History* (Oxford: Oxford University Press, 1999), p. 51.
60. Hippolytus, *Treatise on Christ and Antichrist*, sec. 28, translated in *Ante-Nicene Fathers*, Vol. 5, p. 210.
61. Martin Luther, *The Table Talk of Martin Luther*, trans. and ed. by William Hazlett (London: H.G. Bohn, 1857), p. 327.

Unlike the earlier empires of Daniel's prophecies, the Roman Empire was never conquered in a single battle. Rather, it slowly weakened over the course of several centuries until AD 476, the year generally accepted by historians to mark the fall of the Western Roman Empire (the eastern empire centered in Constantinople survived for another 1,000 years). In this year, the Germanic ruler Odoacer deposed the boy king Romulus Augustus, last emperor of the Western Roman Empire centered in Rome. After AD 476, Europe was no longer under the control of Rome, but was fragmented into ten tribes represented by the ten toes of Daniel 2, and the ten horns of Daniel 7. The famous American evangelist, Dwight Moody, wrote about this division of Daniel's fourth beast:

Unlike the earlier empires of Daniel's prophecies, the Roman Empire was never conquered in a single battle.

> Then came the Caesars, and founded the empire of Rome—symbolized by the legs of iron—the mightiest power the world had ever known; and for centuries Rome sat on those seven hills, and swayed the scepter over the nations of the earth. And then, in its turn, the Roman power was broken; and the mighty empire split up into ten kingdoms corresponding to the ten toes of the prophetic figure.[62]

One aspect of the fourth iron beast that bothered the prophet Daniel was a "little horn" that arose from

62. Dwight L. Moody, *Men God Challenged* (Chicago: Moody Publishers, 1998), p. 15.

among the ten European kingdoms after the division of the Western Roman Empire.

> I was considering the horns, and there was another horn, a little one, coming up among them, before whom three of the first horns were plucked out by the roots. And there, in this horn, were eyes like the eyes of a man, and a mouth speaking pompous words (Daniel 7:8).

This little horn would be different from the fourth beast's ten other horns (Daniel 7:24), but how would it be different? The angel explained to Daniel that this little horn would become "exceedingly great," and seek to expand its territory even "to the host of heaven" (Daniel 8:9–10). It would "cast truth down to the ground" (Daniel 8:12) and "speak pompous words against the Most High" (Daniel 7:25). In other words, the little horn power would be different from normal political powers, or horns, because *it would also exhibit religious characteristics and claim spiritual authority.* The early Christians understood these prophecies, and they identified the little horn power with another ominous character in Bible prophecy—the antichrist. Hippolytus wrote, "the other little horn that grows up among them [the ten horns of the fourth beast] meant the Antichrist in their midst."[63]

Even though the word "antichrist" appears only in the short letters of 1 John and 2 John, it is actually described under numerous names in both the Old and New Testament. These names include the little

63. Hippolytus, *Treatise on Christ and Antichrist*, sec. 28, translated in *Ante-Nicene Fathers*, Vol. 5, p. 210.

horn (Daniel 7 and 8), the beast (Revelation 13), the man of sin, the son of perdition, the mystery of iniquity, and the lawless one (2 Thessalonians 2). The Bible also identifies Jesus Christ by many names, and since "anti" means both "against" and "in place of," it is not surprising that prophecy identifies this menacing power in different ways. Its numerous names simply reflect different aspects of its character, just as Christ's many names reflect different aspects of His character.

In 1 John 2:18 John states, "even now many antichrists have come" and then he says something even more surprising—"they went out from us" (1 John 2:19). In other words, according to the Bible, the antichrist power involves more than just one person, and it emerges from within Christianity! The apostle Paul agreed. He wrote that the "man of sin" would arise through a "falling away" from biblical Christianity (2 Thessalonians 2:3). It seems hard to believe, but the little horn, or antichrist power, actually arises from *within* Christianity!

Paul went on to explain that, even as he was writing his letter, another power was preventing the antichrist from arising. "For the mystery of iniquity doth already work: only he who now letteth [restrains] will let [restrain], until he be taken out of the way" (2 Thessalonians 2:7, KJV). The early Christians understood Paul exactly. Augustine wrote, "[I]t is not absurd to believe that these words of the apostle, 'Only he who now holdeth, let him hold until he be taken out of the way,' refer to the Roman Empire."[64] Remember, the little horn power emerges *after* AD 476 when the fourth beast, the Roman Empire, fragments into ten pieces. Tertullian, another early Christian, wrote, "[H]e who now hinders must hinder until he be taken out of the way. *What obstacle is there but the Roman state*; the falling away of which, by being scattered into ten kingdoms, shall introduce antichrist."[65] Clearly, the early Christians were familiar with the prophecies of Daniel and Paul, and realized that the pagan Roman Empire, though cruel to Christians in many ways, also acted as a deterrent to the emergence of the antichrist power. According to Daniel's vision, the little horn would arise after the fourth beast, Rome, divided into ten parts. "I was considering the horns, and there was another horn, a little one, coming up among them" (Daniel 7:8). The little horn, or antichrist, would arise *after* the division of the Roman Empire.

Paul also predicted that the antichrist would sit "in the temple of God, showing himself that he is God" (2 Thessalonians 2:4). Contrary to popular opinion, this does not mean that the antichrist power will sit in a literal temple in Jerusalem. The Greek word translated as "temple" in this verse is *naos*, and in his writings Paul consistently, and exclusively, uses that word to describe the Christian church! Steve Wohlberg explains this in his book, *End Time Delusions*:

---

64. Augustine, *The City of God*, bk. 20, ch. 19, par. 3, quoted in Steve Wohlberg, *End Time Delusions* (Shippensburg, PA: Destiny Image Publishers, Inc, 2004), p. 79.
65. Tertullian, *On the Resurrection*, chs. 24–25, quoted in H. Grattan Guiness, *Romanism and the Reformation: From the Standpoint of Prophecy* (Hodder and Stoughton, 1887), pp. 196–197.

> Let's allow Paul to interpret Paul. Did Paul use this same word anywhere else in his writings? Yes. In his letter to the early Corinthians, Paul wrote "to the church of God which is at Corinth" (1 Corinthians 1:2). Then he inquired, "Do you not know that you are the temple [naos] of God and that the Spirit of God dwells in you?" (1 Corinthians 3:16). Here Paul clearly applied the word *naos* to the Christian Church—not a physical temple in Jerusalem. He did the same thing in his letter to the Ephesians. Writing to "the saints who are in Ephesus," Paul said they were all growing "into a holy temple [naos] in the Lord" (Ephesians 1:1; 2:21). In fact, in all of his writings, every time Paul used the word *naos*, he *always applied* it to the Christian Church and never to a rebuilt Israeli temple![66]

What does it mean that the antichrist "sits" in the church, or in the temple of God? When Jesus returned to heaven He "sat down on the right hand of God" (Hebrews 10:12), and He told His disciples that at the second coming they would "see the Son of Man sitting at the right hand of the Power, and coming on the clouds of heaven" (Matthew 26:64). Both of these passages point to the position and power that Jesus Christ possesses. To "sit," therefore, can mean to assume a position of *authority*. According to Bible prophecy, the little horn will emerge from within Christianity in Europe sometime after the fall of the Western Roman Empire in AD 476. It will assume

66. Steve Wohlberg, *End Time Delusions* (Shippensburg, PA: Destiny Image Publishers, Inc., 2004), pp. 73–74.

both political and religious power, and after "falling away" from Bible truth it will assume authority over the church.

As Martin Luther and the other reformers studied these prophecies, they reached a unanimous conclusion—the little horn, or antichrist, could be none other than the Roman Catholic Church:[67]

> **Martin Luther.** "We here are of the conviction that the papacy is the seat of the true and real Antichrist."[68]
>
> **John Calvin.** "Some persons think us too severe and censorious when we call the Roman pontiff Antichrist…I shall briefly show that (Paul's words in II Thess. 2) are not capable of any other interpretation than that which applies them to the Papacy."[69]
>
> **Thomas Cranmer.** "Whereof it followeth Rome to be the seat of antichrist, and the pope to be very antichrist himself. I could prove the same by many other scriptures, old writers, and strong reasons."[70]

---

67. It is well to remember that many of the Protestant reformers were originally Roman Catholics themselves, and it is the author's belief that these statements were made not against individual Catholics but rather in reference to a religious system and institution that they believed had slowly drifted from the truth of God's Word, and from which they sincerely desired to call people back to the truth. These quotes and the analysis that follows in subsequent chapters are presented in this spirit.
68. Quoted in Leroy Froom, *Faith of Our Fathers*, vol. 2, p. 121; quoted in Steve Wohlberg, *End Time Delusions*, pp. 90–91.
69. John Calvin, *Institutes of the Christian Religion*, vol. 2, (London: Reinolde Wolfe & Richards Harison, 1561), p. 410; quoted in Steve Wohlberg, *End Time Delusions*, p. 91.
70. *Works by Cranmer*, vol. 1, pp. 6–7, n.p., n.d.; quoted in Steve Wohlberg, *End Time Delusions*, p. 91.

Roger Williams. "[T]he pretended Vicar of Christ on earth, who sits as God over the Temple of God, exalting himself not only above all that is called God, but over the souls and consciences of all his vassals, yea over the Spirit of Christ, over the Holy Spirit, yea, and God himself...speaking against the God of heaven, thinking to change times and laws; but he is the son of perdition (II Thess. 2)."[71]

As Martin Luther and the other reformers studied these prophecies, they reached a unanimous conclusion—the little horn, or antichrist, could be none other than the Roman Catholic Church.

John Wesley. "He is in an emphatic sense, the Man of Sin, as he increases all manner of sin above measure. And he is, too, properly styled the Son of Perdition, as he has caused the death of numberless multitudes, both of his opposers and followers...He it is...that exalteth himself above all that is called God, or that is worshipped...claiming the highest power, and highest honor...claiming the prerogatives which belong to God alone."[72]

71. Quoted in Leroy Froom, *The Prophetic Faith of Our Fathers*, vol. 3, p. 52; quoted in Steve Wohlberg, *End Time Delusions*, pp. 91–92.
72. John Wesley, *Antichrist and His Ten Kingdoms*, p. 110, n.p., n.d.; quoted in Steve Wohlberg, *End Time Delusions*, p. 92.

Cotton Mather. "The oracles of God foretold the rising of an Antichrist in the Christian Church: and in the Pope of Rome all the characteristics of that Antichrist are so marvelously answered that if any who read the Scriptures do not see it, there is a marvelous blindness upon them."[73]

Westminster Confession of Faith. "There is no other head of the church but the Lord Jesus Christ. Nor can the pope of Rome in any sense be head thereof; but is that Antichrist, that man of sin and son of perdition that exalteth himself in the church against Christ and all that is called God."[74]

The identification of the little horn power became a central pillar of the Protestant Reformation. "To the Reformers Rome was the 'Babylon' of the Apocalypse, and the Papal pontiff the predicted 'man of sin.' Separation from the Church of Rome and from its pontifical head was regarded by them as a sacred duty...To them separation from Rome was not separation from Christ, but from antichrist. This was the principle upon which they *began* and *prosecuted* the work of the Reformation, the principle which directed and supported them, and rendered them invincible."[75]

---

73. Cotton Mather, *The Fall of Babylon,* quoted in Leroy Froom, *The Prophetic Faith of Our Fathers,* vol. 3, p. 113; quoted in Steve Wohlberg, *End Time Delusions*, p. 92.
74. *The Westminster Confession of Faith* (1647); quoted in Steve Wohlberg, *End Time Delusions*, p. 92.
75. Henry Grattan Guiness, *Romanism and the Reformation: From the Standpoint of Prophecy*, p. 228.

The Protestant reformers were not the first to express concern about the "spirit of antichrist" that obfuscated Christ's priestly authority in heaven with that of a human priesthood. When the Patriarch of Constantinople assumed the title of "universal" priest, Pope Gregory the Great (AD 590–604) shared his concern in a letter to Emperor Mauricius Augustus:

> Whosever calls himself, or desires to be called, Universal Priest, is in his elation the precursor of Antichrist, because he proudly puts himself above all others. Nor is it by dissimilar pride that he is led into error; for, as that perverse one wishes to appear as God above all men, so whosoever this one is who covets being called the sole priest, he extols himself above all other priests.[76]

Despite Pope Gregory's warning, the pope of Rome himself eventually assumed the title of "universal priest" and the absolute authority accompanying that position. Prophecy predicts that the antichrist power would speak "blasphemies" (Revelation 13:5) and "pompous words against the Most High" (Daniel 7:25). The Bible provides two clear definitions for blasphemy—claiming equality with God (John 10:30–33) and the power to forgive sins (Mark 2:7). Statements from popes and other Roman Catholic sources reveal consistent references to the supposed divinity of the pope:

> **Christopher Marcellus, addressing Pope Julius II (1512).** "Take care that we lose not that salvation,

---

76. Pope Gregory the Great, "Letter to Emperor Mauricius Augustus," in *Epistles*, bk. 7, letter 33, trans. in *Nicene and Post-Nicene Fathers*, ser. 2, vol. 12, 2nd pagination, p. 226.

that life and breath which thou hast given us, for thou art our shepherd, thou art our physician, thou art our governor, thou art our husbandman, *thou art finally another God on earth*."[77]

Pope Leo XIII (1894). "We the pope hold upon this earth the place of God Almighty."[78]

***The Catholic National* (1895).** "The pope is not only the representative of Jesus Christ, but *he is Jesus Christ, Himself*, hidden under the veil of flesh."[79]

Cardinal Sarto, later Pope Pius X (1896). "The Pope represents Jesus Christ Himself."[80]

Pope John Paul II (1995). "Have no fear when people call me the 'Vicar of Christ,' when they say to me 'Holy Father,' or 'Your Holiness,' or use titles similar to these, which seem even inimical to the Gospel."[81]

Bishop Patrick Dunn (2004). "It seems that Pope John Paul II now presides over the universal Church from his place upon Christ's cross."[82]

---

77. Alexander Hislop, *The Light of Prophecy Let in on the Dark Places of the Papacy* (London: William Whyte and Co., 1846): p. 91.
78. Pope Leo XIII, "The Reunion of Christendom," (June 20, 1894), trans. in *The Great Encyclical Letters of Pope Leo XIII* (New York: Benziger, 1903), p. 304.
79. *The Catholic National* (July 1895), emphasis added.
80. *Publications of the Catholic Truth Society*, vol. 29 (Catholic Truth Society: 1896): 11.
81. Pope John Paul II, *Crossing the Threshold of Hope* (New York: Alfred A. Knoff. 1995), p. 6.
82. "Auckland Bishop Says Pope Presides from the Cross," *Zenit* (September 20, 2004), http://1ref.us/l8 (accessed August 14, 2017).

The Roman Catholic Church also claims power for all its priests to forgive sins:

> "Does the Priest truly forgive the sins, or does he only declare that they are remitted? The Priest does really and truly forgive the sins in virtue of the power given to him by Christ."[83]

In his book *The Dignities and Duties of the Priest*, Alphonsus Ligouri explained the priest's assumed power to forgive sins:

> The priest has the power of the keys, or the power of delivering sinners from hell, of making them worthy of paradise, and of changing them from the slaves of Satan into the children of God. And God Himself is obliged to abide by the judgment of His priests, and either not to pardon or to pardon, according as they refuse or give absolution...
>
> Were the Redeemer to descend into a church, and sit in a confessional to administer the sacrament of penance, and a priest to sit in another confessional, Jesus would say over each penitent, "Ego te absolve," the priest would likewise say over each of his penitents, "Ego te absolve," and the penitents of each would be equally absolved...
>
> "Let the priest," says St. Laurence Justinian, "approach the altar as another Christ."[84]

---

83. Joseph Deharbe, *A Complete Catechism of the Catholic Religion* (New York: Schwartz, Kirwin & Fauss, 1924), p. 279.
84. St. Alphonsus de Liguori, *The Dignities and Duties of the Priest* (Potosi, WI: St. Athanasius Press, 2009), pp. 22–29 (reprint).

The Roman Church's numerous and enduring claims of priestly authority led the reformers, and many after them, to identify the Bible's prophetic antichrist power with the papal power. Claims of equality with God and assumptions of power to forgive sins, however, are largely abstract ideas; they result in power only to the extent that people believe and accept them. They are spiritual claims that exist in the religious realm. The prophecy of Daniel 7, however, predicts that the antichrist power would be a little *horn*—that is, it would also possess political power, just like any other empire or kingdom. The keystone of papal authority combined Rome's claims of spiritual supremacy with the power to control civil society. How did the Roman Church obtain its power over civil society? The story is a fascinating one, and it is to this subject that we now turn.

[These] numerous and enduring claims of priestly authority led the reformers, and many after them, to identify the Bible's prophetic antichrist power with the papal power.

The Rest of the Story

"There remains therefore a rest for the people of God."
Hebrews 4:9

For the first three centuries of its existence, the Christian church was regarded first as an offshoot of Judaism, and then later, as a cult that refused to participate in Rome's national religion of emperor worship. During this time Christians faced lesser or greater degrees of marginalization, ridicule, and persecution. One of the bloodiest periods of persecution began in AD 303, when the emperor Diocletian began a ten-year campaign to wipe out Christianity. Christians were stripped of their legal status and removed from public office; their property was seized, and many were put to death.

All this changed, however, when Constantine came to power in AD 312. When he entered Rome as conqueror, he broke with tradition and credited the

Christian God for his victory, rather than offer sacrifices to the pagan Roman gods. The Edict of Milan legalized Christianity in AD 313, and state persecution against the church suddenly came to an end. Confiscated property was returned, and the Lateran Palace was donated to the previously impoverished bishop of Rome.

For centuries, the Roman emperors had been regarded as leaders of the state religion, and this relationship did not change under Constantine. "As the Roman emperor was Pontifex Maximus of the pagan State religion, he [Constantine] would naturally assume the same relation to Christianity when it became predominant. This headship the gratitude of the Christians heartily accorded."[85] Constantine's influence over Christianity became increasingly apparent as time went on. When a dispute regarding ordination arose between two factions of African bishops in AD 313, the emperor stepped in as judge to settle the argument. In AD 325, Constantine summoned the Council of Nicaea, where a number of important doctrinal and ecclesiastical decisions were made. The Council constructed the first part of the Nicene Creed, settled the issue of Jesus Christ's divine nature, and completed an early compilation of canon law. In addition to these accomplishments, however, the Council also prohibited celebration of the Lord's Supper on the day before the Jewish Passover and established the Roman Julian calendar rather than the Hebrew calendar as official for church use. Under Constantine's patronage and protection,

---

85. Albert Henry Newman, *A Manual of Church History*, vol. 1, rev. ed. (Philadelphia: The Judson Press, 1933), p. 307.

Christianity was moving further away from its Jewish and scriptural heritage, and closer to the customs and practices of pagan Rome.

Despite Constantine's magnanimous attitude towards the church, it is unclear whether he ever fully understood or embraced Christianity. His coins, at least until middle age, retained the figures and emblems of pagan gods, and well into his reign he decreed that soothsayers should be consulted if lightning struck the palace or any other public building.[86] Constantine's father, Constantius Chlorus, "professed to have *Sol Invictus* [the 'Invincible Sun'] as [his] special protector and ancestor,"[87] and the historian Edward Gibbon points out that "the devotion of Constantine was... [also] peculiarly directed to the genius of the Sun."[88] Furthermore, the "Christian emperor" ordered his son Crispus to be executed by strangulation, had his second wife Fausta murdered in a bathtub, and was not baptized until lying on his deathbed.

Given all of this, it seems probable that Constantine's interest in Christianity went little further than the security and unity of the empire: "In all of his dealings with Christian matters the supreme motive seems to have been that of securing unity. About doctrinal differences he was almost indifferent. But he dreaded dissension among those on whom he depended for the

---

86. Theodosian Code 16.10.1, trans. by Clyde Pharr (Princeton, NJ: Princeton University Press, 1952), p. 472
87. Franz Cumont, *Astrology and Religion Among the Greeks and Romans* (New York: Dover Publications, Inc., 1960), p. 55 (reprint).
88. Edward Gibbon, *The History of the Decline and Fall of the Roman Empire*, ed. by J.B. Bury, chap. 20, Vol. 2 (London: Methuen & Co., 1896), p. 291.

support of his government."[89] As Charles Cochrane points out in *Christianity and Classical Culture*,

> What he [Constantine] saw in Christianity was simply a talisman by virtue of which *Romanitas* [the Roman political system] would be assured of material prosperity such as official paganism had failed to give it; and, as an uninterrupted series of successes appeared to vindicate this hope, he came more and more to identify the promise of the Evangel with that of the empire and of his own house.[90]

Constantine's triangulation of the Roman political system, paganism, and Christianity was most strikingly achieved with a decree that would forever alter the course of Christianity and ultimately determine how millions worship. In AD 321 Constantine decreed that the "venerable day of the sun," Sunday, should be a day of rest for all citizens. The decree stated:

In AD 321 Constantine decreed that the "venerable day of the sun," Sunday, should be a day of rest for all citizens.

> On the venerable Day of the sun let the magistrates and people residing in cities rest, and let all workshops be closed. In the country, however, persons engaged in agriculture may freely and lawfully continue their pursuits: because it often happens that another Day is not so suitable for grain sowing or for vine planting:

89. Albert Henry Newman, *A Manual of Church History*, vol. 1, rev. ed. (Philadelphia: The Judson Press, 1933), p. 307.
90. Charles Norris Cochrane, *Christianity and Classical Culture* (Oxford: Clarendon Press, 1940), p. 215.

> lest by neglecting the proper moment for such operations the bounty of heaven should be lost.[91]

The decree proved to be a brilliant maneuver for Constantine, for it effectually unified paganism and Christianity under the power of the throne.

Sun worship had long played an important part in Roman paganism. In AD 274, the emperor Aurelian formally introduced sun worship into the Roman Empire. Under Aurelian, "*Sol Invictus* [the 'Invincible Sun'] was definitively promoted to the highest rank in the divine hierarchy and became the official protector of the Sovereigns and of the Empire."[92] By the fourth century the pagan priesthood commonly regarded the sun as the supreme deity, and "Sun-worship was the final form which Roman paganism assumed."[93]

The sun-worshipping cult of Mithraism became particularly influential, and strangely paralleled Christianity in a number of ways. Devotees of Mithraism purified themselves by baptism, participated in a type of "Lord's supper" for salvation of body and soul, believed in the existence of heaven and hell, placed a great flood at the beginning of history, assigned divine revelation as a source of their religious traditions, and looked forward to the resurrection of the dead and a last judgment.[94] In *Paganism to Christianity in*

---

91. Philip Schaff, *History of the Christian Church,* vol. 3 (Edinburg: T&T Clark, 1884), p. 380, note.
92. Franz Cumont, *Astrology and Religion Among the Greeks and Romans* (New York: Dover Publications, Inc., 1960), p. 55 (reprint).
93. Ibid., p.74 (reprint).
94. Franz Cumont, *Astrology and Religion Among the Greeks and Romans* (New York: Dover Publications, Inc., 1960), pp. 190–191 (reprint).

the Roman Empire, Walter Hyde reveals the influence that Mithraism, through Constantine's Sunday law, would have upon Christianity:

> Parallel to the Church movement...but independent of it another had been developing in the State which after an obscure past culminated in Constantine's decree of 321 when the observance of the "day of the Sun" was imposed on the Empire, a decree marking an epoch in the history of Sunday as the beginning of both civil and later of ecclesiastical legislation. Now *dies Solis,* sacred in various solar cults and notably in Mithraism, was to play a role as the Christian Sunday.[95]

A stricter version of Constantine's Sunday law was enacted several decades later at the Council of Laodicea (AD 364–380). This decree prohibited worship on the "Jewish Sabbath" and mandated that Christians work on the seventh day of the week:

> Christians shall not Judaize and be idle on Saturday, but shall work on that day; but the Lord's day they shall especially honor, and, as being Christians, shall, if possible do no work on that day. If, however, they are found Judaizing, they shall be shut out from Christ.[96]

In the span of a few decades, Christianity had moved from a persecuted minority religion to a

95. Walter Woodburn Hyde, *Paganism to Christianity in the Roman Empire* (Philadelphia: University of Pennsylvania Press, 1946), p. 260.
96. Council of Laodicea, canon 29, quoted in A.T. Jones, *Great Empires of Prophecy* (Review and Herald Publishing Association, 1898), p. 486.

powerful state-supported church with the authority to dictate how, and when, people worshipped. Much of the medieval papacy's authority and power over civil society can be traced back to Constantine's Sunday law. The ability to enforce Sunday sacredness formed the bedrock of power on which the authoritative claims of the medieval papacy were built:

> Constantine did many things to favor the bishops. He made their decisions in disputed cases final, as the decision of [the divinity of] Jesus Christ. But in nothing that he did for them did he give them power over those who did not belong to the church, to compel them to act as though they did, except in the one thing of the Sunday law. In the Sunday law, power was given to the church to compel those who did not belong to the church, and who were not subject to the jurisdiction of the church, to obey the commands of the church. *In the Sunday law there was given to the church control of the civil power, so that by it she could compel those who did not belong to the church to act as though they did. The history of Constantine's time may be searched through and through, and it will be found that in nothing did he give to the church any such power, except in this one thing—the Sunday law.*[97]

About now you may be asking, "Why make such a big deal about Constantine's Sunday law? Hasn't Sunday always been the Christian Sabbath?" This is an important question. Let's look in the Bible for an answer.

---

97. A.T. Jones, *Great Empires of Prophecy* (Review and Herald Publishing Association, 1898), pp. 491–492.

The concept of a weekly day of rest originates in the Genesis creation account. According to Scripture, God created the "heavens and the earth" in six days, and "on the seventh day God ended His work which He had done, and He rested on the seventh day from all His work which He had done" (Genesis 2:1–2). "Sabbath" literally means "rest," and the Bible says that God blessed and sanctified, or set apart as holy, this first Sabbath rest day as a memorial of His finished work of creation. This is why the fourth commandment begins with a call to *remember* the seventh-day Sabbath rest. "Remember the Sabbath day, to keep it holy… For in six days the Lord made the heavens and the earth, the sea, and all that is in them, and rested the seventh day. Therefore the Lord blessed the Sabbath day and hallowed it" (Exodus 20:8, 11).

Of course, God's rest on the seventh day of creation was not from weariness, for the Bible says that God "neither faints nor is weary" (Isaiah 40:28). Instead, God established the Sabbath rest to be a blessing for all of humanity, a fact Jesus reminded the Jews about when He said, "The Sabbath was made for *man*" (Mark 2:27, emphasis added). Two thousand years before there was a Jew, God rested from His work of Creation and set apart a holy day for the benefit of the human race. The blessings of the seventh-day Sabbath were never intended just for Israel. On the contrary, God's purpose was that Israel would teach other peoples and nations about this memorial of God's creation.

> Also the sons of the foreigner who join themselves to the LORD, to serve Him, and to love the name of

> the LORD, to be His servants—everyone who keeps from defiling the Sabbath, And holds fast My covenant—even them I will bring to My holy mountain, and make them joyful in My house of prayer. Their burnt offerings and their sacrifices will be accepted on My altar; For My house shall be called a house of prayer for all nations (Isaiah 56:6–7).

The book of Isaiah concludes with a promise that in the new earth, all people will worship God every Sabbath. "'And it shall come to pass that from one New Moon to another, and from one Sabbath to another, all flesh shall come to worship before Me,' says the Lord" (Isaiah 66:23).

Most Christians observe Sunday as a memorial of Christ's resurrection, a tradition that does not find support in the Bible. Scripture contains no reference to a change in the Sabbath, and the New Testament clearly states that God's moral law, of which the seventh-day Sabbath is a part, was actually established by Christ's death. Paul wrote, "Do we then make void the law through faith? Certainly not! On the contrary, we establish the law" (Romans 3:31).

Jesus said that His death and resurrection would have no impact on the continuing authority of God's holy Ten Commandment law upon humanity. "Do not think that I came to destroy the Law or the Prophets. I did not come to destroy but to fulfill. For assuredly, I say to you, *till heaven and earth pass away, one jot or one tittle will by no means pass from the law till all is fulfilled*" (Matthew 5:17–18, emphasis added). We intuitively know that this is true—it is no more lawful in God's sight today to worship false gods, murder, lie, or commit adultery, than it was before the cross. Yet many Christians assume that God's blessing and sanctification of the seventh day was strangely removed or changed to another day following Christ's resurrection. The famous preacher Dwight L. Moody recognized the irony of this position:

> The Sabbath was binding in Eden, and it has been in force ever since. This fourth commandment begins with the word "remember," showing that the Sabbath already existed when God wrote this law on the tables of stone at Sinai. How can men claim that this one commandment has been done away with when they will admit that the other nine are still binding?[98]

Many Christians assume that God's blessing and sanctification of the seventh day was removed or changed to another day following Christ's resurrection.

There is a simple yet profound reason why the Bible indicates no change in the holiness and sacredness of the seventh-day Sabbath as a memorial of God's creative work: The Sabbath is a sign of God's power to redeem us and create new spiritual life in sinners. The same God that created the world through the power of His Word can also create new spiritual life through the power of that same Word. "Moreover I also gave them My Sabbaths, to be a sign between them and

98. Dwight L. Moody, *Weighed and Wanting* (Chicago: Revell, 1898), pp. 46, 47.

Me, that they might know that I am the Lord who sanctifies them" (Ezekiel 20:12).

During His earthly ministry, Jesus indicated the continuing validity and importance of the Sabbath, even after His death. Speaking to His disciples about the coming destruction of Jerusalem by the Romans (which didn't happen until AD 70), Jesus urged them to "pray that your flight may not be in winter or on the *Sabbath*" (Matthew 24:20, emphasis added). The question, of course, is which day was Jesus referring to? Was it the seventh day or the first day of the week?

A survey of the New Testament reveals no direct command from Jesus, the disciples, or the early church leaders authorizing a change of the day of worship from the seventh day to the first day of the week. In the early New Testament church, both Jewish and Gentile Christians worshipped on the Sabbath. "But when they departed from Perga, they came to Antioch in Pisidia, and went into the synagogue on the Sabbath day and sat down…So when the Jews went out of the synagogue, *the Gentiles begged that these words might be preached to them the next Sabbath*" (Acts 13:14, 42). Notice that it was the *Gentiles* that asked Paul to return and preach the next Sabbath. The New Testament mentions over eighty worship services conducted by the early church, and they all occurred on the seventh-day Sabbath.[99]

Since the Bible indicates no change to or cessation of the seventh-day Sabbath, then why do most Christians

99. See Acts 13:14, 42; 16:12–13; 17:1–2; 18:1, 4, 11.

observe Sunday, the first day of the week? *The Convert's Catechism of Catholic Doctrine* provides the answer:

> **Q. Which is the Sabbath day?**
> A. Saturday is the Sabbath day.
>
> **Q. Why do we observe Sunday instead of Saturday?**
> A. We observe Sunday instead of Saturday because *the Catholic Church transferred the solemnity from Saturday to Sunday.*[100]

According to the Roman Catholic Church, it established Sunday sacredness through its own power and authority. The Saint Catherine Catholic Church *Sentinel* reminded its readers of this in 1995:

> Perhaps the boldest thing, the most revolutionary change the Church ever did, happened…[when] [t]he holy day, the Sabbath, was changed from Saturday to Sunday. "The Day of the Lord" (*Dies Dominica*) was chosen, *not from any directions noted in the Scriptures, but from the Church's sense of its own power.*[101]

For hundreds of years, Protestant scholars have repeatedly confirmed this history:

> **Sir William Domville (Church of England).** "Centuries of the Christian era passed away before the Sunday was observed by the Christian church as a Sabbath. History does not furnish us with a single proof or indication that it was at any time so

100. Peter Geiermann, *The Convert's Catechism of Catholic Doctrine* (St. Louis: B. Herder Book Co., 1946), p. 50, emphasis added.
101. *Sentinel* (Algonac, MI: Saint Catherine Catholic Church, May 21, 1995), emphasis added.

observed previous to the Sabbatical edict of Constantine in AD 321."[102]

Dr. R.W. Dale (Congregational). "It is quite clear that however rigidly or devoutedly we may spend Sunday, we are not keeping the Sabbath...The Sabbath was founded on a specific Divine command. We can plead no such command for the obligation to observe Sunday...There is not a single sentence in the New Testament to suggest that we incur any penalty by violating the supposed sanctity of Sunday...The only similarity between the Lord's Day and the Sabbath is that both recur once a week, and that both are religious festivals."[103]

Dr. Augustus Neander (Episcopalian). "The festival of Sunday, like all other festivals, was always only a human ordinance, and it was far from the intentions of the apostles to establish a divine command in this respect, far from them, and from the early apostolic church, to transfer the laws of the Sabbath to Sunday."[104]

---

102. Sir William Domville, *The Sabbath; or, An Examination of the Six Texts,* (London: Chapman and Hall, 1849, p. 291, quoted in Colin Standish and Russell Standish, *The Lord's Day* (Rapidan, VA: Hartland Publications, 2002), p. 56.
103. R.W. Dale, *The Ten Commandments*, (London: Hodder and Stoughton, 1895), pp. 100–101, quoted in Colin Standish and Russell Standish, *The Lord's Day* (Rapidan, VA: Hartland Publications, 2002), p. 57.
104. Augustus Neander, *General History of the Christian Religion and Church*, trans. H.J. Rose, p. 186; quoted in Colin Standish and Russell Standish, *The Lord's Day* (Rapidan, VA: Hartland Publications, 2002), p. 56.

Dr. Edward T. Hiscox (Baptist). "Of course, I know quite well that Sunday did come into use in early Christian history as a religious day, as we learn from the Christian Fathers, and other sources. But what a pity that it comes branded with the mark of paganism, and christened with the name of the sun god, when adopted and sanctioned by the papal apostasy, and bequeathed as a sacred legacy to Protestantism!"[105]

The Confession of the Swiss Church. "The observance of the Lord's Day [Sunday] is founded not on any command of God, but *on the authority of the church*."[106]

According to the Bible, most Christians worship on a day blessed and sanctified by man, not by God. According to the Bible, most Christians worship on a day that points to man's authority, not God's. And according to the Bible, the issue of God's authority versus man's authority lies at the heart of the last

[A]ccording to the Bible, the issue of God's authority versus man's authority lies at the heart of the last great battle between good and evil that will take place on earth just before Jesus Christ returns.

105. Edward Hiscox, Address to a New York Ministers' Conference on November 13, 1893, quoted in Colin Standish and Russell Standish, *The Lord's Day* (Rapidan, VA: Hartland Publications, 2002), p. 56.
106. *The Confession of the Swiss Churches*, quoted in Colin Standish and Russell Standish, *The Lord's Day* (Rapidan, VA: Hartland Publications, 2002), p. 57, emphasis added.

great battle between good and evil that will take place on earth just before Jesus Christ returns. The Bible refers to this battle as the mark of the beast.

A Deadly Wound Healed

"Those who cannot remember the past
are condemned to repeat it."[107]
George Santayana

In Revelation 13, John sees a strange and terrifying beast rise from the sea. "Then I stood on the sand of the sea. And I saw a beast rising up out of the sea, having seven heads and ten horns, and on his horns ten crowns, and on his heads a blasphemous name" (Revelation 13:1). This strange beast resembles a leopard, a bear, and a lion, and it possesses "great authority" (Revelation 13:2). Numerous similarities exist between the sea beast of Revelation 13 and the fourth beast of Daniel 7:

107. George Santayana, *The Life of Reason* (Charles Scribner's Sons: New York, 1905), p. 284.

- Both beasts have 10 horns (Daniel 7:7; Revelation 13:1).
- Both beasts blaspheme God and speak "great words" (Daniel 7:8; Revelation 13:5–6).
- Both beasts make war against God's saints (Daniel 7:25; Revelation 13:7).
- Both beasts rule for the same length of time (Daniel 7:25; Revelation 12:6, 14; Revelation 13:5).

We have already seen that the reformers unanimously agreed that the little horn of Daniel 7 points to the rise of the medieval papal power in Europe. Following this biblical logic, the sea beast of Revelation 13 must also point to this same power.

In Daniel 7, the little horn rules for "a time and times and half a time" (verse 25), or three-and-a-half years. Revelation says that the beast exercises its power for forty-two months (Revelation 11:2 and 13:5) or 1,260 days (Revelation 11:3 and 12:6). A biblical prophetic year equals 360 days, so 1,260 days and forty-two months both refer to this same prophetic three-and-a-half-year period. Does the Bible, then, predict a relatively short period of three-and-a-half literal years in which the little horn would reign? No. In Bible prophecy, a prophetic day almost always represents a literal year. God used this formula when sentencing Israel to forty years in the wilderness (Numbers 14:34) and when instructing Ezekiel to lie on his side for Judah's sins (Ezekiel 4:6). According to this principle, 1,260 days actually points to 1,260 years of rule by the little horn, or sea beast. Does history record a 1,260-year period of papal power in Europe?

In the fourth century Constantine legalized Christianity and brought it under protection of the state. Through the Sunday law he gave the emerging Roman Catholic Church authority and power over the civil government, and for the next 200 years the Church grew in power and influence. In AD 533 the emperor Justinian issued a decree establishing the Roman bishop, or pope, as head of all the western Christian churches. The decree appointed "John, the most holy Archbishop and Patriarch of the noble city of Rome…as being the head of all the churches."[108] Justinian was "zealous for the increase of the honor and authority of your see in all respects,"[109] and this included the ability of the pope to influence and control affairs of the state.

There was just one problem. In AD 533, Rome was under the control of Germanic invaders called the Ostrogoths, and the pope could not effectively exercise the authority Justinian had granted him. Five years later, however, the Ostrogoths abandoned their siege of Rome, and the pope was finally able to begin exercising power over the state. The year AD 538, then, marks the beginning of true papal power, and for the next 1,260 years the papacy was intimately connected with, and often controlled, the politics of Western Europe. During this time period the Church

---

108. *Codex Justiniani,* lib. 1, tit. 1; trans. R.F. Littledale, *The Petrine Claims*, p. 293; quoted in Uriah Smith, *Daniel and the Revelation* (Nashville, TN: Southern Publishing Association, 1944), p. 275.
109. Ibid.

frequently enforced its decrees through the power of the state.

Ancient church documents refer to all the popes prior to the sixth century as "saints." Pope Vigilius, however, who held office in AD 538, "is the first of a series of popes who no longer bear this title, which is henceforth sparingly conferred. From this time on the popes, more and more involved in worldly events, no longer belong solely to the Church; they are men of the state, and then *rulers* of the state."[110] According to Bible prophecy, this church-state union would exist for the next 1,260 years. At times, the power of the state would be stronger, and at other times the power of the church would prevail, but the two would remain united.

The Bible predicts that at the end of the 1,260 years the papacy would receive a "deadly wound" that would make it appear "as it were wounded to death" (Revelation 13:3). One-thousand two-hundred and sixty years after AD 538 reaches to AD 1798. In 1796, French troops under the command of Napolean Bonaparte had invaded Italy and defeated the papal army. Peace ensued for several months, but on December 28, 1797, a French soldier was killed during a riot in Rome. In response, the French army, led by General Berthier, marched into Rome on February 10, 1798, and demanded that Pope Pius VI surrender his temporal, or civil, authority. When the pope refused, Berthier took the pope captive and carried him in

---

110. Charles Bemont, Gabriel Monod, and George Burton Adams, *Medieval Europe from 395 to 1270* (New York: Henry Holt and Company, 1906), pp. 120–121, emphasis added.

exile to Valence, France, where the pope died a year later. The pope's capture effectively dealt a "deadly wound" to the papacy's political power in Europe, and provided a striking fulfillment of the prophecy in Revelation 13:3.

The papacy's loss of political power would not be permanent, however. The Bible makes an astounding prediction in Revelation 13. After receiving its "deadly wound" in 1798, the beast power will eventually regain its lost prestige and influence. Here's how the Bible describes it:

After receiving its "deadly wound" in 1798, the beast power will eventually regain its lost prestige and influence.

> And I saw one of his heads as if it had been mortally wounded, and his deadly wound was healed. And all the world marveled and followed the beast. So they worshiped the dragon who gave authority to the beast; and they worshiped the beast, saying, "Who is like the beast? Who is able to make war with him?" …It was granted to him to make war with the saints and to overcome them. And *authority* was given him over every tribe, tongue, and nation (Revelation 13:3–4, 7, emphasis added).

As it was during the middle ages, the question of spiritual and political authority will be a huge one at the end of time.

In 1929 Italy signed the Lateran Treaty with the Vatican. This treaty established Vatican City as a sovereign state and granted the pope full independence.

Ever since then the Roman Catholic Church has sought to establish itself as a global religious and political authority. In 1967 Pope Paul VI wrote, "Who can fail to see the need and importance of thus gradually coming to the establishment of a *world authority* capable of taking effective action on the juridical and political planes?"[111] His appeal was recently echoed by Pope Benedict XVI, who called for a "radical rethinking of the global economy," and urged "the establishment of a *'true world political authority'* to oversee the economy and work for the 'common good.'"[112]

In 1990, Malachi Martin, a professor at the Pontifical University in Rome, outlined the Vatican's aim to establish itself as the ultimate world authority.

> Willing or not, ready or not, we are all involved in an all-out, no-holds-barred, three-way global competition. Most of us are not competitors, however. We are the stakes. For the competition is about who will establish the first one-world system of government that has ever existed in the society of nations. *It is about who will hold and wield the dual power of authority and control over each of us as individuals and over all of us together as a community.*[113]

Martin identified the three players in this competition as communism, capitalism, and the Vatican,

---

111. Pope Paul VI, *Populorum Progressio*, par. 78 (1967), http://1ref.us/l9 (accessed August 14, 2017).
112. Rachel Donadio and Laurie Goodstein, "Pope Urges New World Economic Order to Work for the 'Common Good,'" *The New York Times* (7 July 2009), emphasis added, http://1ref.us/la (accessed August 14, 2017).
113. Malachi Martin, *The Keys of this Blood* (Touchstone: New York, 1990), p. 15, emphasis added.

and pointed to the uniqueness of the Roman Catholic Church's claims of authority.

> The primary difficulty for Pope John Paul II in both of these models [communism and capitalism] for the new world order is that neither of them is rooted in the *moral laws of human behavior revealed by God through the teaching of Christ, as proposed by Christ's church…This is the backbone principle of the new world order envisaged by the Pontiff.*[114]

In the Vatican's view neither communism nor capitalism can provide a viable solution to the world's many problems because both of them are inherently secular. Instead, the world needs a religious power, such as the Vatican, that can exercise not only political power but also enforce *moral laws and moral authority*. Near the end of his exposé Martin reiterated that "the [Vatican's] goal is a geopolitical structure for the society of nations designed and maintained according to the ethical plans and *doctrinal outlines of Christianity as taught by the Roman Pontiff* as the earthly Vicar of Christ."[115]

Follow the argument carefully. According to Malachi Martin, during the last century the Vatican has carefully and methodically established itself as a world authority with "a diplomatic style that relie[s] principally on *moral status*, not political weight, or even on its financial clout. It [has] developed to a high degree the Catholic sense of the papacy as the

114. Malachi Martin, *The Keys of this Blood* (Touchstone: New York, 1990), p. 19, emphasis added.
115. Ibid., p. 455, emphasis added.

ultimate arbiter for problems and dilemmas affecting nations all over the globe."[116]

The papacy's role as "ultimate arbiter" has been increasingly noticeable in recent years. In late 2014 *Time* magazine reported that a personal letter written by Pope Francis to Barack Obama and Raúl Castro played a significant role in opening up negotiations and "normaliz[ing] relations" between the United States and Cuba.[117] A few months later, on June 18, 2015, the Vatican released *Laudato Si*, Pope Francis' much-awaited encyclical on solutions to the world's environmental problems. The document, which was intentionally worded to address "every person living on this planet,"[118] captured the attention of religious, scientific, and political leaders around the world. United States President Barack Obama responded by saying that he welcomed the encyclical, and "deeply admire[d] the Pope's decision to make the case…with the full *moral authority* of his position."[119]

That moral authority was put on full display three months later in September 2015, when Pope Francis visited the United States and made an unprecedented speech before Congress. In that speech the pope called for action on issues ranging from immigration, the death penalty, and racial injustice, to the weapons

---

116. Malachi Martin, *The Keys of this Blood* (Touchstone: New York, 1990), p. 136, emphasis added.
117. Zeke Miller and Elizabeth Dias, "How Pope Francis Helped Broker Cuba Deal," *Time* (17 December 2014), http://1ref.us/lb (accessed August 14, 2017).
118. Pope Francis, *Laudato Si,* par. 3 (24 May 2015), http://1ref.us/lc (accessed August 14, 2017).
119. Barack Obama, "Statement by the President on Pope Francis' Encyclical," (18 June 2015), http://1ref.us/ld (accessed August 14, 2017).

trade and poverty. Many people saw the pope's visit as "a real opportunity for the Catholic Church here in America to reclaim a level of *moral authority* that's been lost"[120] due to factors such as rising secularism and the clergy sex-abuse scandals.

Barack Obama is not the only world leader to make reference to the pope's moral authority. When Soviet president Mikhail Gorbachev met Pope John Paul II in 1989, he introduced his wife to the pope by saying, "Raisa Maximovna, I have the honor to introduce the highest *moral authority* on earth."[121] Shortly after his election as President of the United States, George W. Bush remarked that "the best way to honor Pope John Paul II, truly one of the great men, is to take his teaching seriously; is to listen to his words and put his words and teachings into action here in America. This is a challenge we must accept."[122]

More recently, Shimon Peres, former prime minister of Israel, pointed to Pope Francis as the world's best authority to provide moral guidance. He said, "So given that the United Nations has run its course, what we need is an organization of United Religions...What we need is an unquestionable *moral authority* who says out loud, 'No. God doesn't want this and doesn't allow it.'" Peres then suggested Pope Francis as the best

120. Lisa Wangsness, "Pope has chance to reclaim 'moral authority' in visit," *The Boston Globe* (23 September 2015), emphasis added, http://1ref.us/le (accessed August 14, 2017).
121. Steven Gertz, "What part did Pope John Paul II play in opposing Communism in Eastern Europe?" *Christianity Today* (8 August 2008), emphasis added, http://1ref.us/lf (accessed August 14, 2017).
122. George W. Bush, Speech to delegation of U.S. Catholic cardinals at White House (21 March 2001), http://1ref.us/m3 (accessed August 24, 2017).

person to head this kind of world body, because "perhaps for the first time in history, the Holy Father is a leader who's respected, not just by a lot of people, but also by different religions and their representatives."[123]

The Bible predicts that a single global moral authority will eventually materialize, and that worship laws and the enforcement of the mark of the beast will follow.

> He was granted power to give breath to the image of the beast, that the image of the beast should both speak and cause as many as would not worship the image of the beast to be killed. He causes all, both small and great, rich and poor, free and slave, to receive a mark on their right hand or on their foreheads, and that no one may buy or sell except one who has the mark or the name of the beast, or the number of his name (Revelation 13:15–17).

The papal power during the middle ages exercised "great authority" (Revelation 13:2), and *authority* will be a hallmark of the revived papacy at the end of time. What is the mark of moral authority that it will enforce on the world? Keep reading to find out!

The Bible predicts that a single global moral authority will eventually materialize, and that worship laws and the enforcement of the mark of the beast will follow.

123. "Pope Francis more powerful advocate for peace than U.N., Shimon Peres proclaims," *Catholic Online* (5 September 2014), emphasis added, http://1ref.us/lg (accessed August 14, 2017).

The Mark of Authority

"It is impossible to keep men together in one religious denomination, whether true or false, except they be united by means of visible signs or sacraments."[124]
Augustine of Hippo

The warning about the mark of the beast is God's most solemn warning in Scripture. It's so important that prophecy depicts an angel flying through heaven with an urgent message to avoid this deadly mark:

> Then a third angel followed them, saying with a loud voice, "If anyone worships the beast and his image, and receives his mark on his forehead or on his hand, he himself shall also drink of the wine of the wrath of God, which is poured out full strength

124. Augustine, quoted in Thomas Aquinas, "Treatise on the Sacraments," question 61, art. 1, *Summae Theologica,* http://1ref.us/lh (accessed August 14, 2017).

> into the cup of His indignation. He shall be tormented with fire and brimstone in the presence of the holy angels and in the presence of the Lamb" (Revelation 14:9–10).

Clearly, it is important to understand what this mark is, and how to avoid it! The Bible reveals a number of important things about the mark of the beast. We will identify four of the most important here:

1. The mark belongs to the *beast* (Revelation 14:9). We have seen that the Bible clearly identifies this beast as Daniel's little horn power, and that the Protestant reformers and many others through history understood these symbols as pointing to the papal power. The mark, therefore, must be something that belongs to the Roman Catholic Church.
2. The mark involves *worship* (Revelation 13:15; 14:9).
3. The mark involves *authority*, for its acceptance is enforced on all people (Revelation 13:16).
4. The mark can be placed on the *forehead* or the *hand* (Revelation 13:16; 14:9).

Before identifying the mark of the beast, we must understand that it is simply a counterfeit to the seal of God. At the end of time, all people will receive one of these two marks. Just as bank tellers study real money in order to identify counterfeit bills, the best way to recognize the counterfeit seal, or mark, at the end of time is to know what the real one is. In Revelation 7:1–3, John sees four angels holding back four winds of strife from blowing on the earth while God's servants are sealed. Like the mark of the beast, the seal of God is placed on the forehead.

> Then I saw another angel ascending from the east, having the seal of the living God. And he cried with a loud voice to the four angels to whom it was granted to harm the earth and the sea, saying, "Do not harm the earth, the sea, or the trees till we have sealed the servants of our God on their foreheads" (Revelation 7:2–3).

How are God's servants sealed? According to the Bible, it's the Holy Spirit that performs this important work. Paul told the church in Ephesus, "you were sealed with the Holy Spirit of promise" (Ephesians 1:13). The Bible explains the Holy Spirit's sealing work by comparing it to an author's writing. "Clearly you are an epistle of Christ, ministered by us, written not with ink but by the Spirit of the living God, not on tablets of stone but on tablets of flesh, that is, of the heart" (2 Corinthians 3:3). You have no doubt written some important documents in your life, but this is a writing assignment that only God can accomplish! What does the Holy Spirit write on the hearts of God's servants? "I will put My laws in their mind and write them on their hearts; and I will be their God, and they shall be My people" (Hebrews 8:10).

God's servants are sealed as the Holy Spirit writes God's law on their hearts. This should not be surprising, for Psalm 19:7 tells us, "The law of the Lord is perfect, converting the soul." Many people have never thought of God's law, the Ten Commandments, as a good thing. They've always seen it instead as just so many rules. "Don't do this, don't do that." The Bible, however, urges us to view God's law as a wall of protection and a shield against sin. "Your word have I hidden in my heart, that I might not sin against You," wrote David in Psalm 119:11. God's law, when written on the mind and heart, becomes not just a list of "dos and dont's," but a way of life that ties us to our Redeemer. Says God, "Bind up the testimony, seal the law among my disciples" (Isaiah 8:16).

In the Old Testament, God gave the Israelites a tangible way to show that His law was in their hearts, that they recognized God's authority in their lives. "And these words which I command you today shall be in your heart…You shall bind them as a sign on your hand, and they shall be as frontlets between your eyes" (Deuteronomy 6:6, 8). He instructed them to literally attach copies of His law to their hands and foreheads—exactly the same places that Revelation 13 says the mark of the beast is placed!

The seal of God is contained in God's law, the Ten Commandments. Only one of the Ten Commandments deals specifically with worship and God's authority, and that is the fourth commandment. God instructs all mankind to worship him on the seventh day in recognition of His authority as Creator.

> Remember the Sabbath day, to keep it holy. Six days you shall labor and do all your work, but the seventh day is the Sabbath of the Lord your God.

God instructs all mankind to worship him on the seventh day in recognition of His authority as Creator.

In it you shall do no work: you, nor your son, nor your daughter, nor your male servant, nor your female servant, nor your cattle, nor your stranger who is within your gates. For in six days the Lord made the heavens and the earth, the sea, and all that *is* in them, and rested the seventh day. Therefore the Lord blessed the Sabbath day and hallowed it (Exodus 20:8–11).

Any king or monarch has a royal seal that identifies who they are. When the president of the United States speaks, for instance, a round seal is placed in front of him identifying his name, title, and territory. The Sabbath commandment likewise contains God's divine seal of authority:

1. His name ("the LORD thy God"),
2. His title (Creator, implied by the phrase, "the LORD [Who] made"),
3. and His territory ("heaven and earth, the sea, and all that in them is").

God specifically told the Israelites that the seventh-day Sabbath is His chosen sign of power and authority. It is the seal of God! "Surely My Sabbaths you shall keep, *for it is a sign between Me and you* throughout your generations, that you may know that I am the Lord who sanctifies you." (Exodus 31:13, emphasis added). Even the Roman church recognizes this. In 2001, the Pontifical Biblical Commission plainly stated that the seventh-day Sabbath points to God's authority:

> ...human existence is endowed with a certain rhythm. As well as the rhythm of day and night, lunar months and solar years (Gen. 1:14–18), *God establishes a weekly rhythm with rest on the seventh day*, the basis of the sabbath (Gen. 2:1–3). *When they keep the sabbath observance* (Ex 20:8–11), *the masters of the earth render homage to their Creator.*[125]

If God's authority is recognized by worship on the seventh day of the week, then how is man's authority recognized? In 1923, the *Catholic Record* provided the answer:

> The Bible still teaches that the Sabbath or Saturday should be kept holy. There is no authority in the New Testament for the substitution of Sunday for Saturday. Surely it is an important matter. It stands there in the Bible as one of the Ten Commandments of God. There is no authority in the Bible for abrogating this Commandment, or for transferring its observance to another day of the week...The Church is above the Bible, and this transference of Sabbath observance from Saturday to Sunday is proof positive of that fact. *Deny the authority of the Church and you have no adequate or reasonable explanation or justification for the substitution of Sunday for Saturday.*[126]

---

125. The Pontifical Biblical Commission, *The Jewish People and Their Sacred Scriptures in the Christian Bible*, sec. 27 (2001), emphasis added, http://1ref.us/li (accessed August 14, 2017).
126. *Catholic Record* (1 September 1923), p. 4, emphasis added.

This is not an isolated claim of the Church's authority in regards to Sunday worship. The following statements, all from Roman Catholic sources, clearly reveal that it regards Sunday as the sign, or mark, of its power and authority.

> Protestants...accept Sunday rather than Saturday as the day for public worship after the Catholic Church made the change...But the Protestant mind does not seem to realize that...in observing the Sunday, they are accepting the authority of the spokesman to the church, the Pope.[127]

> It is well to remind the Presbyterians, Baptists, Methodists, and all other Christians, that the bible does not support them anywhere in their observance of Sunday. Sunday is an institution of the Roman Catholic Church, and those who observe the day observe a commandment of the Catholic Church.[128]

> All things whatsoever that it was duty to do on the Sabbath, these we [the Church] have transferred to the Lord's day, as being more authoritative and more highly regarded and first in rank, and more honorable than the Jewish Sabbath.[129]

> The Divine institution of a day of rest from ordinary occupations and of religious worship, transferred by the authority of the Church from the

127. *Our Sunday Visitor* (5 February 1950).
128. Priest Brady, in an address, reported in the Elizabeth, N.J. *News* (18 March 1903).
129. Eusebius, *Commentary on the Psalms* on Ps. 91 (92): 2, 3, in *Patrologia Graeca*, J.P. Migne, ed., vol. 23, col. 1172.

Sabbath, the last day, to Sunday, the first day of the week, ...is one of the most patent signs that we are a Christian people.[130]

Q. Have you any other way of proving that the Church has power to institute festivals of precept?
A. Had she not such power, she could not have done that in which all modern religionists agree with her;—she could not have substituted the observance of Sunday the first day of the week, for the observance of Saturday the seventh day, a change for which there is no Scriptural authority.[131]

It was the Catholic Church which, by the authority of Jesus Christ, has transferred this rest of the Sunday in remembrance of the resurrection of our Lord. Thus the observance of Sunday by the Protestants is an homage they pay, in spite of themselves, to the authority of the [Catholic] church.[132]

"Of course the Catholic church claims that the change was her act. And the act is a mark of her ecclesiastical power and authority in religious matters."[133]

---

130. Cardinal James Gibbons, "The Claims of the Catholic Church in the Making of the Republic," in John Gilmary Shea, et. al., *The Cross and the Flag, Our Church and Country* (New York: The Catholic Historical League of America, 1899), pp. 24–25.
131. Stephen Keenan, *A Doctrinal Catechism,* 3rd American ed., rev. (New York: T.W. Strong, late Edward Dunigan & Bro., 1876), p. 174.
132. Louis Gaston de Ségur, *Plain Talk About the Protestantism of To-day* (Boston: Patrick Donaho, 1868), p. 225.
133. Extract from letter written by C.F. Thomas, Chancellor of Cardinal Gibbons (11 November 1895).

Remember that, according to Malachi Martin, the "backbone principle of the new world order envisaged by the Pontiff" is a "society of nations" rooted in the "*moral laws of human behavior*" specifically "*as proposed by Christ's church*."[134] The current *Catholic Catechism* identifies Sunday observance as the fulfillment of the moral law: "*The celebration of Sunday observes the moral commandment* inscribed by nature in the human heart to render to God an outward, visible, public, and regular worship 'as a sign of his universal beneficence to all.' *Sunday worship fulfills the moral command…*"[135]

The mark of the beast, like the seal of God, is entirely an issue of authority—*do I accept God's authority or man's authority in my life*? At the end of time, all people living on earth will have to decide whose authority to accept, and this decision will be revealed by whom they obey. "Do you not know that to whom you present yourselves slaves to obey, you are that one's slaves whom you obey, whether of sin leading to death, or of obedience leading to righteousness?" (Romans 6:16). The mark of the beast—the legal enforcement of Sunday sacredness and the prohibition of seventh-day Sabbath observance—will be a test of authority in *worship*, a

At the end of time, all people living on earth will have to decide whose authority to accept, and this decision will be revealed by whom they obey.

134. Malachi Martin, *The Keys of this Blood* (Touchstone: New York, 1990), pp. 19, 455, emphasis added.
135. *Catechism of the Catholic Church*, par. 2176, http://1ref.us/lj (accessed August 14, 2017).

perfect counterfeit of God's seal of authority found in the fourth commandment.

The Bible indicates that God's law as expressed in the Ten Commandments will still be in force at the end of time. In Revelation John sees in vision a group of people that are loyal to God in the face of great trial and persecution. "And the dragon was enraged with the woman, and he went to make war with the rest of her offspring, *who keep the commandments of God* and have the testimony of Jesus Christ" (Revelation 12:17, emphasis added). Two chapters later John sees this same group of people again. "Here is the patience of the saints; here are *those who keep the commandments of God* and the faith of Jesus" (Revelation 14:12, emphasis added). Finally, in the last chapter of the Bible, John sees the Tree of Life and those that are given access to it again. "*Blessed are those who do His commandments*, that they may have the right to the tree of life, and may enter through the gates into the city" (Revelation 22:14, emphasis added).

The evidence of Scripture and history, and the words of the Catholic Church itself, reveal that God has never removed or changed His blessing from the seventh-day Sabbath. It still points us back to God's authority as Creator. The Roman Catholic Church, through its union with state power, established legally-enforced Sunday worship, and this day points to that Church's authority. Today, Sunday worship remains a memorial of Roman power and authority, and it is increasingly advocated as the one thing that can unite Christianity once again. Strangely, many Protestants agree with Rome's claims.

The Lord's Day Alliance is an ecumenical, inter-denominational organization whose stated purpose is "to encourage all people to recognize and observe a day of Sabbath rest and to worship the risen Lord Jesus Christ, on the Lord's Day, Sunday."[136] In April 2015, the organization published an article on its website titled, "Sunday as a Mark of Christian Unity." The article argued that Sunday worship is a "marker of Christian unity" and concluded by pointing to Sunday worship as Christianity's greatest visible sign, or mark, of unity.

> In order to fully appreciate *Sunday as a mark of Christian unity* we must expand our definition of unity…When we assemble in faith on Sundays, we gather not simply with other parishioners in a local place of worship, but with Christians throughout every land and all the ages—*and there is no greater evidence of unity than this*.[137]

The papacy's ultimate goal, however, is not simply to have all Christians worshipping together on Sunday. Rather, the "end game" is to have all of Christendom recognize and submit to papal authority. As Pope Leo XIII said, "[T]he supreme teacher in the Church is the Roman Pontiff. Union of minds, therefore, requires, together with a perfect accord in the one faith, *complete submission and obedience of will to the Church and to the Roman Pontiff, as to God*

---

136. http://1ref.us/lk (accessed August 14, 2017).
137. Demetrios Tonias, "Sunday as a Mark of Christian Unity," emphasis added, http://1ref.us/ll (accessed August 14, 2017).

Himself.[138] The real issue is the re-establishment of an absolute spiritual and civil authority.

In May of 1998 the Vatican released two documents that revealed this agenda. The first, released on May 18, was an addition to the *Code of Canon Law* which stated:

> Whoever denies a truth which must be believed with divine and catholic faith, or who calls into doubt, or who totally repudiates the Christian faith, and does not retract after having been legitimately warned, is to be punished as a heretic or an apostate with a major excommunication.[139]

The ruling concluded by warning that "whoever obstinately rejects a teaching [of] the Roman Pontiff or the College of Bishops…and does not retract after having been legitimately warned, is to be punished with an appropriate penalty."[140] Under church-state unity in the middle ages, the "appropriate penalty" for those that disagreed with the pope was death. Augustine, the "father of Catholic theology," defined the church's position toward heretics:

> Though heretics must not be tolerated because they deserve it, we must bear with them, till, by a second admonition, they may be brought back to the faith of the church. But those who after a second

---

138. Pope Leo XIII, "On the Chief Duties of Christians as Citizens," 10 January 1890, trans. in *The Great Encyclical Letters of Pope Leo XIII* (New York: Benziger, 1903), p. 193, emphasis added.
139. Pope John Paul II, *Ad Tuendam Fidem*, canon 1436, art. 1 (18 May 1998), http://1ref.us/lm (accessed August 14, 2017).
140. Pope John Paul II, *Ad Tuendam Fidem*, canon 1436, art. 2 (18 May 1998), http://1ref.us/lm (accessed August 14, 2017).

> admonition, remain obstinate in their errors, must not only be excommunicated, but they must be delivered to the secular power to be exterminated.[141]

To this day the definition of heresy remains the same. The 2000 edition of the *American Heritage Dictionary* defines a heretic as "a person who holds controversial opinions, especially one who publicly dissents from the officially accepted dogma of the Roman Catholic Church."[142]

A few days after these additions were made to the *Code of Canon Law*, Pope John Paul II issued his encyclical *Dominus Dei* ("The Day of the Lord"). The encyclical made a plea for Sunday sacredness and argued that civil laws need to protect and enforce its observance: "Therefore, also in the particular circumstances of our own time, Christians will naturally strive to ensure that civil legislation respects their duty to keep Sunday holy."[143] In 2007 Pope Benedict XVI repeated John Paul's argument, calling again for civil legislation to protect Sunday sacredness:

> Sunday thus appears as the primordial holy day, when all believers, wherever they are found, can become heralds and guardians of the true meaning of time…Finally, it is particularly urgent nowadays to remember that the day of the Lord is also a day of rest from work. *It is greatly to be hoped that this*

---

141. Thomas Aquinas, *Summa Theologica*, vol. 4, p.90; quoted in Charles Paschal Chiniquy, *Fifty Years in the Church of Rome,* 43rd ed., rev. (New York: Fleming H. Revell Company, 1886), p. 676.
142. "Heretic," *The American Heritage Dictionary*, 4th ed., (2000).
143. Pope John Paul II, *Dies Domini,* ch. 4, par. 67 (31 May 1998), http://1ref.us/ln (accessed August 14, 2017).

> *fact will also be recognized by civil society*, so that individuals can be permitted to refrain from work without being penalized.[144]

In 2015, Pope Francis released his encyclical on the environment. Unlike most papal encyclicals, it was anticipated and received with great interest not just by Catholics, but also by scientists, politicians, and thought leaders around the world. The document addressed environmental challenges facing society, and concluded with a surprising solution for protecting Earth, its inhabitants, and the environment—the protection of Sunday sacredness: "Sunday, like the Jewish Sabbath, is meant to be a day which heals our relationships with God, with ourselves, with others and with the world."[145] Ironically, the Bible presents the seventh-day Sabbath as God's solution to these same problems:

> If you turn away your foot from the Sabbath, From doing your pleasure on My holy day, And call the Sabbath a delight, The holy day of the Lord honorable, And shall honor Him, not doing your own ways, Nor finding your own pleasure, Nor speaking your own words, Then you shall delight yourself in the Lord; And I will cause you to ride on the high hills of the earth, And feed you with the heritage of Jacob your father. The mouth of the Lord has spoken (Isaiah 58:13–14).

---

144. Pope Benedict XVI, *Sacramentum Caritatis*: *Post-Synodal Apostolic Exhortation on the Eucharist as the Source and Summit of the Church's Life and Mission,* paragraphs 73–74 (22 February 2007), emphasis added, http://1ref.us/lo (accessed August 14, 2017).
145. Pope Francis, *Laudato Si,* par. 237 (24 May 2015), http://1ref.us/lc (accessed August 14, 2017).

The Bible clearly identifies the seventh-day Sabbath as God's seal of authority. As its counterfeit, the mark of the beast points to Sunday sacredness as the sign of man's presumed authority. How will the mark of the beast be enforced and Sunday sacredness made into law? We will see the Bible's answer to that question in the next chapter.

The Bible clearly identifies the seventh-day Sabbath as God's seal of authority. As its counterfeit, the mark of the beast points to Sunday sacredness as the sign of man's presumed authority.

A Friend in Strange Places

"With the Sabbath our Christianity and our country stand or fall. A republic cannot endure without morality, nor morality without religion, nor religion without the Sabbath, nor the Sabbath without law."[146]
Wilbur Crafts

According to the Bible, the papacy will not recover from its "deadly wound" and enforce the mark of the beast on its own. Instead, a powerful and unexpected ally—a second beast—will come to its aid. The Bible describes this second beast:

Then I saw another beast coming up out of the

146. Wilbur F. Crafts, "The Manifold Worth of the Sabbath", *Our Day*, vol. 8, issues 1-3 (Boston, 8th ed.), July 1891, at 23, quoted in Bethany Rupert, "The Sunday Rest Bill and the Battle to Keep the Civil Sabbath," *Seton Hall Legislative Journal* vol. 39:2, p. 286, http://1ref.us/lp (accessed August 14, 2017).

> earth, and he had two horns like a lamb and spoke like a dragon. And he exercises all the authority of the first beast in his presence, and causes the earth and those who dwell in it to worship the first beast, whose deadly wound was healed (Revelation 13:11–12).

Four clues in this passage reveal the identity of the beast that rises from the earth:

1. **It appears around the year 1798.** According to prophecy, this second beast, or political power, emerges at the end the papacy's 1,260 years of rule. This time prophecy ended in 1798, when the papacy received its deadly wound and was "killed with the sword" (Revelation 13:10). The very next verse, Revelation 13:11, pictures the second beast arising from the earth immediately after the papacy receives its "deadly wound." Bible students understood the proximity of these two events before they happened; in 1754 John Wesley wrote, "He [the beast from the earth] is not yet come, though he cannot be far off; for he is to appear at the end of the forty two months of the first beast."[147]
2. **It comes "up out of the earth."** Since "water" in prophecy refers to people and nations (Isaiah 17:12; Revelation 17:15), "earth" must represent an unpopulated area. The last time

147. John Wesley, *Explanatory Notes on the New Testament* (London: W. Bowyer, 1754), pp. 753–754, notes.

"earth" was mentioned was in Revelation 12:15–16, where the earth opens its mouth to protect the woman (God's people) from papal persecution. Therefore, "earth" must refer to a relatively unpopulated area of the world around the year 1798 that offered religious freedom.

3. **It has "two horns like a lamb."** Revelation repeatedly uses a lamb to symbolize Christ (Revelation 5:6). Therefore, this new nation must profess Christianity. Also, there are no crowns on its horns, signifying that no king rules here. In contrast, the sea beast, or Papacy, has ten crowns on its seven heads, indicating the presence of kingly power.

4. **It attains global power and economic influence.** The beast from the earth grows in strength to eventually exert worldwide influence (he "deceives them," Revelation 13:14), military power ("he causes all," Revelation 13:16) and economic strength ("that no one may buy or sell," Revelation 13:17).

Only one power in the world matches the four prophetic descriptions of the second beast in Revelation 13. The United States declared its independence in 1776, won its freedom in 1783, and implemented its Constitution in 1787. It arose in a relatively unpopulated area of the world and was founded as a nation free from monarchical control and that offered religious freedom. Today it exercises global power and economic influence as the world's only true superpower.

The United States was built on the twin principles of religious and civil freedom. These are represented in the "two horns" without crowns, and for more than two centuries the Constitution and Bill of Rights have protected these freedoms. For nearly 250 years freedom for millions has been guaranteed by the separation of power—not only the separation of executive, congressional, and judicial power, but of religious and civil power as well. This heritage is enshrined in the Constitution and Bill of Rights, and attested to in official congressional documents:

> The framers of the Constitution recognized the eternal principle that man's relation with his God is above human legislation, and his rights of conscience inalienable. Reasoning was not necessary to establish this truth; we are conscious of it in our own bosoms. It is this consciousness which, in defiance of human laws, has sustained so many martyrs in tortures and flames. They felt that their duty to God was superior to human enactments, and that man could exercise no authority over their consciences. It is an inborn principle which nothing can eradicate.[148]

Thomas Jefferson, the third president of the United States, once wrote to a group of Baptists in Danbury, Connecticut, about the importance of separating the powers of church and state, and of allowing all people freedom of conscience in matters of religion. His attitude reveals the principles on which the

---

148. Congressional documents (U.S.A.), serial No. 200, document No. 271, quoted in Ellen G. White, *The Great Controversy* (Boise, ID: Pacific Press Publishing Association, 1911), p. 295.

United States was founded.

> Believing with you that religion is a matter which lies solely between Man & his God, that he owes account to none other for his faith or his worship, that the legitimate powers of government reach actions only, & not opinions, I contemplate with sovereign reverence that act of the whole American people which declared that their legislature should "make no law respecting an establishment of religion, or prohibiting the free exercise thereof," thus building a wall of separation between Church & State.[149]

These principles of individual freedom and the separation of church and state powers diametrically oppose the papacy's unchanging claims to spiritual and civil authority, and its historical reliance on church and state unity. This difference was not lost on America's early leaders.

In a letter written in 1821 to Thomas Jefferson, John Adams wrote, "I have long been decided in opinion that a free government and the Roman Catholick [sic] religion can never exist together in any nation or Country."[150] In another letter, Adams bluntly stated, "Liberty and Popery cannot live together."[151] General

---

149. Thomas Jefferson, "Jefferson's Letter to the Danbury Baptists" (1 January 1802), http://1ref.us/lq (accessed August 14, 2017).
150. Letter from John Adams to Thomas Jefferson, February 3, 1821, in Cappon, *Adams-Jefferson Letters*, 2:571, quoted in James Hutson, *The Founders on Religion: A Book of Quotations* (Princeton, NJ: Princeton University Press, 2005), p. 41.
151. Letter from John Adams to Louisa Catherine Adams, May 17, 1821, in *Adams Papers* (microfilm), reel 451, Library of Congress, quoted in James Hutson, *The Founders on Religion: A Book of Quotations* (Princeton, NJ: Princeton University Press, 2005), p. 41.

Marquis De Lafayette, the French soldier and aristocrat who participated in the French Revolution of the 1790s and helped the United States gain its independence from Britain, said,

> It is my opinion that if the liberties of this country—the United States of America—are destroyed, it will be by the subtlety of the Roman Catholic Jesuit priests, for they are the most crafty, dangerous enemies to civil and religious liberty. They have instigated most of the wars in Europe.[152]

Years later, Abraham Lincoln issued a similarly ominous warning:

> I do not pretend to be a prophet. But though not a prophet, I see a very dark cloud on our horizon. And that dark cloud is coming from Rome. It is filled with tears of blood. It will rise and increase, till its flanks will be torn by a flash of lightning, followed by a fearful peal of thunder. Then a cyclone such as the world has never seen, will pass over this country, spreading ruin and desolation from north to south…Neither I nor you, but our children, will see those things.[153]

As shocking as it may seem, the Bible predicts that the United States will someday discard its long-held principles of civil and religious freedom, reunite the power of church and state, and "[cause] the earth and

---

152. General Marquis De Lafayette, quoted by Rev. Dr. Vanpelt in James L. Chapman, *Americanism versus Romanism: or the cis-Atlantic battle between Sam and the pope* (Nashville, TN, 1856), p. 127.
153. Abraham Lincoln, quoted in Carpenter, *Six Months in the White House*, p. 86, quoted in Charles Chiniquy, *Fifty Years in the Church of Rome* (New York: Fleming H. Revell Company, 1885), p. 715.

those who dwell in it to worship the first beast, whose deadly wound was healed" (Revelation 13:12). The papacy received its "deadly wound" in 1798 when the pope was taken captive and his civil power was broken. The "healing of the wound" can only mean that the papacy will once again wield both spiritual and political influence and power. Revelation 13:3 predicts that after this deadly wound is healed, "all the world marveled and followed the beast." This time the papacy will control not just Europe, but the entire world. In order for this prophecy to be fulfilled, the papacy must have the support and cooperation of the United States, the world's most powerful nation.

As early as 1892 the papacy identified the United States as the partner it needed to regain its lost political power and recover from its "deadly wound." Pope Leo wrote in a letter to the *New York Sun* in 1892,

> "What can we borrow, and what ought we to borrow from the United States for our social, political, and ecclesiastical reorganization?" The answer depends in great measure upon the development of American destinies. If the United States succeed in solving the many problems that puzzle us, Europe will follow her example, and this outpouring of light will mark a date in the history not only of the United States, BUT OF ALL HUMANITY.

As early as 1892 the papacy identified the United States as the partner it needed to regain its lost political power and recover from its "deadly wound."

> That is why the holy father, anxious for peace and strength, collaborates with passion in the work of consolidation and development in American affairs. According to him, the Church ought to be the chosen crucible for the molding and absorption of races into one united family. And that, especially, is the reason why he labors at the codification of ecclesiastical affairs, in order that *this distant member of Christianity [the United States] may infuse new blood into the old organism.*[154]

From the papal perspective, the "old organism" could be nothing other than the medieval church-state alliance that suffered its "deadly wound" in AD 1798. We have already seen that Constantine's Sunday law formed the seed of this original alliance in AD 321, and it is significant that Pope Leo's letter to the *New York Sun* was written shortly after an attempt by the United States Congress to protect Sunday sacredness. In 1888 Senator H.W. Blair introduced the National Sunday-Rest Bill (Senate Bill No. 2983), which read in part:

> [N]o person or corporation, or the agent, servant, or employee of any person or corporation, shall perform or authorize to be performed, any secular work, labor, or business, to the disturbance of others, works of necessity, mercy, and humanity excepted; nor shall any person engage in any play, game, or amusement, or recreation, to the

154. Letter from the Vatican to the *New York Sun* (11 July 1892), quoted in A.T. Jones, *Ecclesiastical Empire* (Battle Creek, MI: Review and Herald Publishing Company, 1901), p. 858.

> disturbance of others, on the first day of the week, commonly known as the Lord's day, or during any part thereof, in any territory, district, vessel, or place, subject to the exclusive jurisdiction of the United States; nor shall it be lawful for any person or corporation to receive pay for labor or service performed or rendered in violation of this section.[155]

The bill was narrowly defeated, but sent signals that the United States was willing to consider laws enforcing Sunday sacredness.

Had it passed, the Blair "Sunday law" bill would have enforced Sunday sacredness on the federal level. However, numerous states already had Sunday closing "blue laws" designed to restrict or ban certain activities on the first day of the week. Many of these "blue laws" still exist on state books, though most haven't been actively enforced for decades. In 1883, five years before Senator Blair introduced his federal "Sunday law" bill, *The American Catholic Quarterly Review* published a revealing article explaining exactly what power lurks behind Sunday sacredness laws.

> Strange as it may seem, the State, in passing laws for the due sanctification of Sunday, is unwittingly acknowledging the authority of the Catholic Church, and carrying out more or less faithfully its prescriptions. *The Sunday, as a day of the week set apart for the obligatory public worship of Almighty God*, to be sanctified by a suspension of all servile labor, trade,

155. Senator H.W. Blair, "National Sunday-Rest Bill," Senate Bill No. 2983, Introduced in First Session of Fiftieth Congress (21 May 1888), http://1ref.us/lr (accessed August 14, 2017).

> and worldly avocations and by exercises of devotion, *is purely a creation of the Catholic Church.*
>
> ...The Catholic Church created the Sunday and made the very regulations which have come down on the statute-books...
>
> Protestantism, in discarding the authority of the Church, has no good reason for its Sunday theory, and ought, logically, to keep Saturday as the Sabbath...For their present practice Protestants in general have no authority but that of a Church which they disown, and there cannot be a greater inconsistency than theirs in asking the state to enforce the Sunday laws.[156]

Despite this inconsistency, the Bible predicts that the United States, historically the bastion of Protestantism and religious freedom, will one day cause "the earth and them which dwell therein to worship the first beast, whose deadly wound was healed" (Revelation 13:12). The "land of the free, and the home of the brave" will unite

The Bible predicts that the United States, historically the bastion of Protestantism and religious freedom, will one day cause "the earth and them which dwell therein to worship the first beast, whose deadly wound was healed" (Revelation 13:12).

156. John Gilmary Shea, "The Observance of Sunday and Civil Laws for Its Enforcement," *The American Catholic Quarterly Review*, 8 (January 1883), pp. 139, 149, and 152, emphasis added.

with Rome and eventually enforce papal dogmas and decrees. This alliance visibly materialized in 1982 when Pope John Paul II and President Ronald Reagan joined forces in the fight against Soviet Union communism, though their secret alliance became public only after the fall of the Berlin Wall in 1989. *Time* magazine broke the story on February 24, 1992, with the electrifying headline, "Holy Alliance: How Reagan and the Pope conspired to assist Poland's Solidarity movement and hasten the demise of communism." The article explained the alliance in detail:

> Only President Ronald Reagan and Pope John Paul II were present in the Vatican Library on Monday, June 7, 1982. It was the first time the two had met, and they talked for 50 minutes…In that meeting, Reagan and the Pope agreed to undertake a clandestine campaign to hasten the dissolution of the communist empire. Declares Richard Allen, Reagan's first National Security adviser: "This was one of the great secret alliances of all time."
>
> … "Nobody believed the collapse of communism would happen this fast or on this timetable," says a cardinal who is one of the Pope's closest aides. "But in their first meeting, the Holy Father and the President committed themselves and the institutions of the church and America to such a goal. And from that day, the focus was to bring it about in Poland." Step by reluctant step, the Soviets and the communist government of Poland bowed to the

> moral, economic and political pressure imposed by the Pope and the President.[157]

The collapse of the Berlin Wall in 1989 signaled the end of the Soviet Union and European communism. It also ushered the world into a new era—an era with only one superpower, the United States of America. Henry Kissinger, Secretary of State under President Ronald Reagan, warned that the change in world politics also signaled a major change must take place within the United States.

> The New World Order cannot happen without U.S. participation, as we are the most significant single component. Yes, *there will be a New World Order, and it will force the United States to change its perceptions*.[158]

In what ways would the United States need to change its perceptions to make an alliance with the Vatican?

First, its historical wariness of "popery," as voiced by John Adams, Abraham Lincoln, and many other early leaders, would need to dissolve. This has already happened. When John F. Kennedy was campaigning for the presidency in 1960, he found it necessary to distance himself from the Church. "I am not the Catholic candidate for President. I am the Democratic Party's candidate for President who happens also to be a Catholic. I do not speak for my church on public matters;

---

157. Carl Bernstein, "The Holy Alliance: Ronald Reagan and John Paul II," *Time* (24 February 1992).
158. Henry Kissinger in *World Affairs Council Press Conference*, Regent Beverly Wilshire Hotel (19 April 1994), emphasis added.

and the church does not speak for me."[159] However, in the run-up to the 2016 presidential election, *Time* magazine asserted that "the golden age of Catholicism in American politics has arrived," and its headline suggested that "Preaching Pope Francis's Politics May Be the Key to Becoming President."[160] With Donald Trump's election this may not immediately seem to be the case, given his vocal opposition to many of the pope's favorite agendas, such as open borders. Any personal friction that may exist between Trump and Pope Francis does not negate the fact, however, that the 2016 presidential election saw "a bumper crop of Catholic candidates"[161] with six of the 17 major GOP candidates identifying themselves as Roman Catholic.

Secondly, the historical separation between church and state powers would need to be eliminated. Like Thomas Jefferson, John F. Kennedy believed in the division of these two powers, and publicly stated, "I believe in an America where the separation of church and state is absolute…I am wholly opposed to the State being used by any religious group, Catholic or Protestant, to compel, prohibit, or prosecute the free exercise of any other religion."[162] Since Kennedy made this statement,

---

159. John F. Kennedy, "Address to the Greater Houston Ministerial Association," *American Rhetoric*, http://1ref.us/ls (accessed August 14, 2017).
160. Christopher J. Hale, "Preaching Pope Francis' Politics May Be the Key to Becoming President," *Time* (24 July 2015), http://1ref.us/lt (accessed August 14, 2017).
161. David Masci, "The 2016 GOP field has a bumper crop of Catholic candidates," Pew Research Center (23 July 2015), http://1ref.us/lu (accessed August 14, 2017).
162. John F. Kennedy, "Address to the Greater Houston Ministerial Association," *American Rhetoric*, http://1ref.us/ls (accessed August 14, 2017).

the separation of church and state in America has come under increasing scrutiny and attack. In 1985, for example, Chief Justice of the Supreme Court William Rehnquist wrote, "The 'wall of separation between church and state' is a metaphor based on bad history, a metaphor which has proved useless as a guide to judging. It should be frankly and explicitly abandoned."[163]

More recently, presidential candidate Rick Santorum repeated Rehnquist's position in more colorful language. In 2011, while speaking at the College of St. Mary Magdalen, the senator and Presidential candidate said, "I almost threw up"[164] after reading Kennedy's 1960 speech on the separation of church and state. When asked to explain his statement some time later, Santorum said, "I don't believe in an America where the separation of church and state is absolute. The idea that the church can have no influence or no involvement in the operation of the state is absolutely antithetical to the objectives and vision of our country."[165] Santorum apparently is not alone. In 2014 the Pew Forum released the results of a survey that found "a growing share of the American public wants religion to play a role in U.S. politics."[166]

President Donald Trump, apparently aware of this growing public sentiment, promised during his campaign that if elected he would "get rid of and totally

---

163. *Wallace v. Jaffree*, 472 U.S. 38, 107 (1985) (Rehnquist, J., dissenting).
164. Rick Santorum, speech at College of St. Mary Magdalen (11 October 2011), http://1ref.us/lv (accessed August 14, 2017).
165. Rick Santorum, interview with George Stephanopoulos, http://1ref.us/lv (accessed August 14, 2017).
166. "Public Sees Religion's Influence Waning," Pew Research Center (22 September 2014), http://1ref.us/lw (accessed August 14, 2017).

destroy the Johnson amendment"[167] that since 1954 has limited the ability of religious tax-exempt organizations to endorse or oppose political candidates. Following Trump's election on November 8, 2016, a coalition of influential "faith leaders and prophets" has formed the POTUS (President of the United States) Shield as "a powerfully interactive spiritual, apostolic, prophetic force."[168] According to its website, the POTUS Shield's purpose is to "discern, declare, and decree the strategies of the Lord for our nation, with a special sensitivity to the three branches of the United States Government."[169]

Clearly, the secularization of America over the past sixty years has led many (though of course not all) people to advocate a restoration of religious values into American life. However, the Bible predicts that this movement will eventually result in a combination of church-and-state power that resembles the religious-political union that gave the papacy so much control of medieval Europe. Revelation calls this union the "image of the beast."

> And he [the second beast, or the United States] deceives those who dwell on the earth by those signs which he was granted to do in the sight of the beast, telling those who dwell on the earth to make an image to the beast who was wounded by the sword and lived. He was granted *power* to give breath to

---

167. Elizabeth Landers, "Trumpet: I will 'destroy' Johnson amendment," *CNN* (2 February 2017), http://1ref.us/lx (accessed August 14, 2017).
168. http://1ref.us/ly (accessed August 14, 2017).
169. Ibid.

the image of the beast, that the image of the beast should both speak and cause as many as would not worship the image of the beast to be killed (Revelation 13:14–15).

The United States, for over 200 years the world's haven of religious and civil freedom, will one day deny its lamb-like appearance and begin speaking "like a dragon" (Revelation 13:11). In Revelation 12 the dragon persecuted those "who keep the commandments of God" (Revelation 12:17), and this persecution will resume when the mark of the beast is enforced. According to Bible prophecy, mandatory observance of Sunday sacredness will be advocated, and eventually enforced, as the solution to the world's many problems. If it still seems unlikely that the United States could ever play a part in this kind of religious coercion, consider the comments that an Arizona state senator made in 2015 during a debate on gun control: "Probably we should be debating a bill requiring every American to *attend a church of their choice on Sunday* to see if we can get back to having a moral rebirth."[170] The great issue at the end of time will be the same as during the Reformation 500 years ago—who has authority to choose how, when, where, and whom, you worship?

Mandatory observance of Sunday sacredness will be advocated, and eventually enforced, as the solution to the world's many problems

170. Nikki Schwab, "Arizona Senator Suggests That Church Be Mandatory," *U.S. News & World Report* (27 March 2015), emphasis added, http://1ref.us/lz (accessed August 14, 2017).

Much like when Daniel lived in ancient Babylon, a showdown is coming between the commandments of God and the commandments of men. When Daniel's enemies devised a law mandating worship of the king and outlawing worship of any other god, Daniel chose to continue acknowledging the authority of the God of heaven. Though thrown into the lion's den for his loyalty to God, Daniel's life was miraculously preserved. The Bible likewise predicts that there will be some who remain loyal to God at the end of time when the mark of the beast is enforced on the earth. Revelation describes these people:

> And I saw something like a sea of glass mingled with fire, and those who have the victory over the beast, over his image and over his mark and over the number of his name, standing on the sea of glass, having harps of God. They sing the song of Moses, the servant of God, and the song of the Lamb, saying: "Great and marvelous are Your works, Lord God Almighty! Just and true are Your ways, O King of the saints! Who shall not fear You, O Lord, and glorify Your name? For You alone are holy. For all nations shall come and worship before You, For Your judgments have been manifested" (Revelation 15:2–4).

Do you want to be among the group that remains loyal to God? You can be. It is possible to avoid the mark of the beast, and to choose to accept God's authority in your life. You only have to answer one question.

Is the Reformation Finished?

"But the path of the just is as the shining light, that shineth more and more unto the perfect day."
Proverbs 4:18

Is the Reformation finished? In the 500 years since Luther nailed his ninety-five theses to the church door, Rome has relinquished none of its authoritative claims and changed none of the doctrines that led to the schism in the sixteenth century. The pope still claims to sit on Peter's throne and exercise the "power of the keys." The Church still teaches that confession must be made to human priests, and acts of penance must be carried out under their direction. Mary is still placed on an unbiblical pedestal and the merit of the saints is still distributed through indulgences. Tradition still sits on an equal footing with the Bible. The Council of Trent's anathemas against those who reject papal authority and teachings of the Church have never been repudiated. In short, the gulf between biblical Christianity and Roman Catholicism remains as wide as it was on the day in 1521 that Martin Luther stood before the diet (council) at Worms and pronounced, "I cannot submit my faith either to the pope or to the councils…Here I stand, I can do no other; may God help me."[171] According to William Webster, a former Roman Catholic-turned evangelical Protestant,

> The issues that separate Protestantism and Roman Catholics are not minor. They are major. They have to do with the eternal destinies of men and women. They hit right at the heart of truth, both biblical and historical. The defining issue is truth…Much of the ecumenical movement of the last fifty years or so would have us downplay the importance of truth for the sake of unity. But the ultimate issue is not unity; it is commitment to Christ. And that means a commitment to truth…If we forsake truth for a man-made unity, we actually forsake Christ![172]

The search for truth fueled the Reformation. In the fourteenth century, John Wycliffe restored the Bible in the vernacular, and the façade of papal authority and supremacy began to tremble. In the sixteenth century, Martin Luther recovered the truth of

---

171. Ellen G. White, *The Great Controversy* (Boise, ID: Pacific Press Publishing Association, 1911), p. 160.
172. William Webster, "Did I Really Leave the Holy Catholic Church?" in *Roman Catholicism*, John Armstrong, ed. (Chicago: Moody Press, 1994), pp. 284–287.

justification by faith alone, and more Roman pillars began to shake as people rediscovered that God's forgiveness and grace comes through the blood of Jesus, not the ministration of sacraments by human priests. Luther's contemporary, John Calvin, pointed to Jesus Christ as the Mediator and Intercessor of mankind, and the curtain of the confessional booth was ripped aside as people learned they could pray directly to their Savior. In the early seventeenth century, John Smyth began teaching and practicing baptism by immersion, pointing to the role of confession and repentance in baptism. With this truth came the realization that baptism represents entrance into God's kingdom of freedom from sin, not the initiation of a contract to obey the Church. The reformers and thousands who have come after them have Biblically and faithfully upheld these truths and taken their stand upon the authority of the Bible and the authority of Jesus Christ, often at the cost of reputation, position, and life itself.

These Biblical truths were not rediscovered all at once; they unfolded over a period of centuries. As the Bible says, "the path of the just *is* like the shining sun, that shines ever brighter unto the perfect day" (Proverbs 4:18). Justification by faith in many ways, and for many good reasons, became the standard of the Protestant Reformation. However, this was not simply the unearthing of one isolated, long-buried doctrine. It was a ray of light illuminating a pathway away from human authority and back to God.

In the words of one nineteenth-century author,

> The Reformation did not, as many suppose, end with Luther. It is to be continued to the close of this world's history. Luther had a great work to do in reflecting to others the light which God had permitted to shine upon him; yet he did not receive all the light which was to be given to the world. From that time to this, new light has been continually shining upon the Scriptures, and new truths have been constantly unfolding.[173]

The Protestant Reformation, however, did nearly die over 450 years ago. As the Reformation spread, concern grew within the Roman Catholic Church that its influence and power would eventually be swept away. Luigi Mocenigo, Venetian ambassador at Rome, wrote of the impact that the Reformation was having on the Roman Catholic Church. "In many countries, obedience to the pope has almost ceased, and matters are becoming so critical that, if God does not interfere, they will soon be desperate."[174]

Things did become desperate enough that a council was called to deal with the issues. The Council of Trent was a series of meetings convened between 1545 and 1563 in which the Church addressed many of the abuses of power that had led to the Reformation. These included grievances in church discipline and administration such as the sale of indulgences, moral

---

173. Ellen G. White, *The Great Controversy* (Boise, ID: Pacific Press Publishing Association, 1911), p. 148.
174. John Hungerford Pollen, "The Counter-Reformation," *The Catholic Encyclopedia*, vol. 4 (New York: Robert Appleton Company, 1908), http://1ref.us/m0 (accessed August 14, 2017).

life within convents, and the education of clergy. The Council also asserted the authority of the pope, condemned the principles and positions of Protestantism, and issued dogmatic declarations defending virtually every doctrine contested by the reformers. The result was a revitalized Roman Catholic Church in many parts of Europe. Yet it almost didn't succeed. The question of authority nearly unraveled the entire Council.

The principle of *sola scriptura*, or "the Bible only," formed the vital backbone of the Protestant Reformation, and many people within the Roman Catholic Church began questioning if the Bible did in fact have more authority than Church tradition. After nearly two decades of meetings, the Council of Trent had not yet provided a clear reason why this mass of writings, and church tradition in general, should be regarded as more authoritative than Scripture. "[T]hus far they had not been able to orient themselves to the interchanging, crisscrossing, labyrinthine, twisting passages of an older and newer concept of tradition."[175] The Protestant position, with its professed reliance on the Bible as a single and ultimate source of authority, appeared to be quite logical in comparison.

The principle of* sola scriptura*, or "the Bible only," formed the vital backbone of the Protestant Reformation.

The Church's answer to this dilemma came in 1562 on the opening day of the last series of meetings.

175. Heinrich Julius Holtzmann, *Kanon und Tradition* (Ludwigsburg: Druck and Verlag von Ferd. Riehm, 1859), p. 263, quoted in Don F. Neufeld and Julia Neuffer, *Seventh-day Adventist Bible Student's Source Book* (Washington, D.C.: Review and Herald Publishing Association, 1962), pg. 888.

This day was the festival of the chair of St. Peter at Rome, a feast established four years earlier by Pope Pius IV to celebrate the power and authority of the Bishop of Rome and the Holy See. The German historian Heinrich Holtzmann tells the story:

> Finally, at the opening of the last session, January 18, 1562, all scruples were cast aside; *the archbishop of Rheggio made a speech, in which he openly declared that tradition stood higher than the Bible.* For this reason alone the authority of the Church could not be bound to the authority of the Scriptures: *because the former had changed the Sabbath into Sunday—not by the commandment of Christ, but solely by her own authority.* This destroyed the last illusion, and it was hereby declared *that tradition signified not so much antiquity, but rather continuing inspiration.*[176]

The bishop continued by reminding the council that it was the Church, not Christ, that had abolished the seventh-day Sabbath and established Sunday sacredness in its stead. "The Sabbath, the most glorious day in the law, has been merged into the Lord's day," he said, "and that solely by the authority of the Church."[177]

The argument was simple and conclusive: The Protestants as a whole did in fact observe Sunday as sacred and, therefore, acknowledged in spite of themselves the authority of the Roman Catholic Church.

---

176. Heinrich Julius Holtzmann, *Kanon und Tradition* (Ludwigsburg: Druck and Verlag von Ferd. Riehm, 1859), p. 263, quoted in A.T. Jones, *Ecclesiastical Empire* (Battle Creek, MI: Review and Herald Publishing Co., 1901), p. 853.
177. Ibid, p. 854.

Don't miss what this means! It was on the Protestant observation of Sunday sacredness that the foundation of Roman Catholic authority was finally defined and defended! Years ago, the *Catholic Mirror* published this stunning admission: "The Protestant world has been, from its infancy, in the sixteenth century, in thorough accord with the Catholic Church, in keeping 'holy,' not Saturday, but Sunday."[178] The article continued by stating,

> The Catholic Church for over one thousand years before the existence of a Protestant, by virtue of her Divine mission, changed the day from Saturday to Sunday... The Protestant world at its birth found the Christian Sabbath too strongly entrenched to run counter to its existence; it was therefore placed under the necessity of acquiescing in the arrangement, thus implying the Church's right to change the day, for over 300 years. The Christian Sabbath is therefore to this day the acknowledged offspring of the Catholic Church, as Spouse of the Holy Ghost, without a word of remonstrance from the Protestant world.[179]

The Roman church rose to power in Constantine's time on the issue of Sunday sacredness, and it essentially neutered the Protestant Reformation on the same issue more than a thousand years later. From Constantine's day until now, Sunday has remained the visible sign of Roman Catholic authority.

---

178. "The Christian Sabbath," *The Catholic Mirror*, vol. XLIV, no. 34 (2 September 1893), p. 8, http://1ref.us/m1 (accessed August 14, 2017).
179. Ibid, pp. 29–31.

The reformation, therefore, remains unfinished. In spite of all the cords of tradition that the Reformers successfully shook off, one last fiber of papal authority remains woven through the faith traditions of mainline Protestants, liberal Protestants, evangelicals, Pentecostals, charismatics, fundamentalists, and thousands of Christians claiming no denomination at all. Sunday sacredness, Rome's openly admitted sign of authority, remains coiled around virtually every Christian church, denomination, and sect. Catholic priest John O'Brien summarized the issue this way:

> But since *Saturday, not Sunday, is specified in the Bible*, isn't it curious that non-Catholics who profess to take their religion directly from the Bible and not from the Church, observe Sunday instead of Sabbath? ...[T]hat observance remains as a reminder of the Mother Church from which the non-Catholic sects broke away—like a boy running away from home but still carrying in his pocket a picture of his mother or a lock of her hair.[180]

The Reformers were adamant that justification comes by grace through faith alone, without the need for "meritorious works" on the part of human beings. Their message of justification was a message of rest in the all-sufficient merits of the blood of Jesus Christ. The seventh-day Sabbath, the memorial of God's work of creation, remains also the sign of His power and authority to re-create a sinful human being in His image. The Bible identifies God's holy day, the

180. John O'Brien, *The Faith of Millions* (Huntington, IN: Our Sunday Visitor, Inc., 1974), pp. 400–401, emphasis added.

seventh-day Sabbath, as the sign of God's completed work of salvation.

> For He has spoken in a certain place of the seventh day in this way: "And God rested on the seventh day from all His works" ...There remains therefore a rest for the people of God. For he who has entered His rest has himself also ceased from his works as God did from His (Hebrews 4:4, 9–10).

Where are the Protestants today? Where are those that will stand on God's chosen sign of authority and shake off the last remaining dust of Roman tradition? Revelation 18 predicts a final revival and reformation of truth that will spread across the world before Jesus Christ returns. "After these things I saw another angel coming down from heaven, having great authority, and the earth was illuminated with his glory." (Revelation 18:1). This angel's message is specific, and urgent:

> And he cried mightily with a loud voice, saying, "Babylon the great is fallen, is fallen, and has become a dwelling place of demons, a prison for every foul spirit, and a cage for every unclean and hated bird! For all the nations have drunk of the wine of the wrath of her fornication, the kings of the earth have committed fornication with her, and the merchants of the earth have become rich through the abundance of her luxury." And I heard another voice from heaven saying, "Come out of her, my people, lest you share in her sins, and lest you receive of her plagues" (Revelation 18:2–4).

Where are the Protestants today? Where are those that will stand with the courage of Luther and cut the final tie that holds them to the authority of Rome? Where are those that will "come out" and stand on the sign of God's authority as Creator and Redeemer? The day God blessed and sanctified on the final day of creation is still blessed and sanctified today. What He spoke from a mountain, engraved on stone, and told us to remember, He still expects us to regard as holy.

This book is a call for all Christians to carefully and prayerfully consider the Bible's claim that the seventh-day Sabbath is God's chosen sign of authority. As Jesus said, "No one can serve two masters; for either he will hate the one and love the other, or else he will be loyal to the one and despise the other" (Matthew 6:24). For fifteen hundred years the light and truth of God's seventh-day Sabbath has been largely forgotten, obscured under the dusty cloud of human traditions and papal authority. It is time to reestablish God's seventh-day Sabbath in its rightful position in the hearts and minds of all Christians, and finish the work of reform begun by Wycliffe, Luther, Calvin, and so many others. It is time to finish the Reformation. It is time to restore the institution God established in Eden, and fully claim His authority over our lives.

The day God blessed and sanctified on the final day of creation is still blessed and sanctified today.

That institution which points to God as the Creator is a sign of his rightful authority over the

> beings he has made. The change of the Sabbath is the sign, or mark, of the authority of the Romish Church. Those who, understanding the claims of the fourth commandment, choose to observe the false in place of the true Sabbath, are thereby paying homage to that power by which alone it is commanded.[181]

Revelation predicts that the world will "wonder after the beast" and "worship" it. The world will, in the end, accept the sign of papal authority, but you don't have to. There is only one question that you need to answer: Will you worship God on His holy day? The final battle still lies ahead. The Reformation is not finished; it has only just begun.

---

181. Ellen G. White, *The Spirit of Prophecy*, vol. 4 (Battle Creek, MI: Review and Herald Publishing Association, 1884), p. 281.

Bibliography

The American Heritage Dictionary, 4th ed. Boston, MA: Houghton-Mifflin, 2000.

Aquinas, Thomas. "Treatise on the Sacraments," question 61, art. 1, *Summae Theologica* (accessed 13 March 2017 at http://1ref.us/lh).

"Article 28." *The Thirty-nine Articles of the Church of England Explained*, 6th ed. London: Methuen & Company, 1908.

Ashley, Jim. "Death of Protestantism Foreseen," *Chattanooga Free Press*, editor's note, May 10, 1997.

"Auckland Bishop Says Pope Presides from the Cross." *Zenit*, September 20, 2004 (accessed August 14, 2017 at http://1ref.us/l8).

Bainvel, Jean. "Tradition and Living Magisterium," *The Catholic Encyclopedia*, vol. 15. New York: Robert Appleton Company, 1912 (accessed August 14, 2017 at http://1ref.us/ks).

Bernstein, Carl. "The Holy Alliance: Ronald Reagan and John Paul II," *Time*, February 24, 1992.

Blair, H.W. "National Sunday-Rest Bill." Senate Bill No. 2983, Introduced in First Session of Fiftieth Congress, May 21, 1888 (accessed August 14, 2017 at http://1ref.us/lr).

Chapman, L. *Americanism versus Romanism: or the cis-Atlantic battle between Sam and the Pope.* Nashville, TN: 1856.

"The Christian Sabbath." *The Catholic Mirror*, vol. XLIV, no. 34, September 2, 1893 (accessed August 14, 2017 at http://1ref.us/m1).

Bemont, Charles, Gabriel Monod, and George Burton Adams. *Medieval Europe from 395 to 1270.* New York: Henry Holt and Company, 1906.

Bush, George W. *Speech to Delegation of U.S. Catholic Cardinals at White House,* March 21, 2001 (accessed August 24, 2017 at http://1ref.us/m3).

The Canons and Decrees of the Sacred and Oecumenical Council of Trent, ed. and trans. by J. Waterworth. London: Dolman, 1848 (accessed August 14, 2017 at http://1ref.us/kv).

Catechism of the Catholic Church (accessed August 14, 2017 at http://1ref.us/m2).

The Catholic National, July 1895.

Catholic Online. September 5, 2014 (accessed August 14, 2017 at http://1ref.us/lg).

Catholic Record. September 1, 1923.

Chamberlain, Gary, and Patrick J. Howell. *Empowering Authority: The Charisms of Episcopacy and Primacy in the Church.* Kansas City, MO: Sheed & Ward, 1990.

Chiniquy, Charles Paschal. *Fifty Years in the Church of Rome,* 43rd ed., rev. New York: Fleming H. Revell Company, 1886.

Church in the U.S.A. *The Protestant Reformation and Its Influence, 1517–1917.* BiblioLife, 2015.

Code of Canon Law. (accessed August 14, 2017 at http://1ref.us/l6)

Cochrane, Charles Norris. *Christianity and Classical Culture.* Oxford: Clarendon Press, 1940.

Crouch, Paul. "Praise the Lord Program." Trinity Broadcasting Network, October 17, 1989.

Cumont, Franz. *Astrology and Religion Among the Greeks and Romans.* New York: Dover Publications, Inc., 1960.

Davis, Paul K. *100 Decisive Battles from Ancient Times to the Present: The World's Major Battles and How They Shaped History.* Oxford: Oxford University Press, 1999.

Deharbe, Joseph. *A Complete Catechism of the Catholic Religion.* New York: Schwartz, Kirwin & Fauss, 1924.

St. Alphonsus de Liguori, St. Alphonsus. *The Dignities and Duties of the Priest.* Potosi, WI: St. Athanasius Press, 2009.

de Ségur, Louis Gaston. *Plain Talk About the Protestantism of Today.* Boston, MA: Patrick Donaho, 1868.

Donadio, Rachel, and Laurie Goodstein, "Pope Urges New World Economic Order to Work for the 'Common Good,'" *The New York Times,* July 7, 2009.

Donovan, Colin B. "Sacraments in Scripture" (accessed August 14, 2017 at http://1ref.us/l0).

Eusebius. *Commentary on the Psalms,* in *Patrologia Graeca*, J.P. Migne, ed., vol. 23, col. 1172.

Geiermann, Peter. *The Convert's Catechism of Catholic Doctrine.* St. Louis, MO: B. Herder Book Co., 1946.

Gertz, Steven. "What Part Did Pope John Paul II Play in Opposing Communism in Eastern Europe?" *Christianity Today,* August 8, 2008 (accessed August 14, 2017 at http://1ref.us/lf).

Gibbon, Edward. *The History of the Decline and Fall of the Roman Empire.* London: Methuen & Co., 1896.

Guiness, Grattan. *Romanism and the Reformation: From the Standpoint of Prophecy.* London: Hodder and Stoughton, 1887.

Hale, Christopher J. "Preaching Pope Francis' Politics May Be the Key to Becoming President," *Time,* July 24, 2015 (accessed August 14, 2017 at http://1ref.us/lt).

Hamm, Berndt. *The Early Luther: Stages in a Reformation Reorientation.* Grand Rapids, MI: William B. Eerdmans Publishing Company, 2010.

Hanna, Edward. "The Sacrament of Penance," *The Catholic Encyclopedia*, vol. 11. New York: Robert Appleton Company, 1911 (accessed August 14, 2017 at http://1ref.us/l2).

Hippolytus. *Treatise on Christ and Antichrist*, sec. 28, translated in *Ante-Nicene Fathers*, Vol. 5.

Hislop, Alexander. *The Light of Prophecy Let in on the Dark Places of the Papacy.* London: William Whyte and Co., 1846.

Hutson, James. *The Founders on Religion: A Book of Quotations.* Princeton, NJ: Princeton University Press, 2005.

Hyde, Walter Woodburn. *Paganism to Christianity in the Roman Empire.* Philadelphia: University of Pennsylvania Press, 1946.

Jefferson, Thomas. "Jefferson's Letter to the Danbury Baptists," January 1, 1802 (accessed August 14, 2017 at http://1ref.us/lq).

Jarret, Bede. "Feudalism," *The Catholic Encyclopedia,* vol. 6. New York: Robert Appleton Company, 1909 (accessed August 14, 2017 at http://1ref.us/ky).

Jones, A.T. *Ecclesiastical Empire.* Battle Creek, MI: Review and Herald Publishing Company, 1901.

Jones, A.T. *Great Empires of Prophecy.* Review and Herald Publishing Association, 1898.

Jones, Michael Keenan. *Jesus Our Priest: A Christian Approach to the Priesthood of Christ.* Oxford: Oxford University Press, 2010.

Keenan, Stephen. *A Doctrinal Catechism,* 3rd American ed., rev. New York: T.W. Strong, late Edward Dunigan & Bro., 1876.

Kennedy, Daniel. "Sacraments," *The Catholic Encyclopedia,* vol. 13. New York: Robert Appleton Company, 1912 (accessed August 14, 2017 at http://1ref.us/ku).

Kennedy, John F. "Address to the Greater Houston Ministerial Association," *American Rhetoric* (accessed August 14, 2017 at hhttp://1ref.us/ls).

Kissinger, Henry. *World Affairs Council Press Conference,* Regent Beverly Wilshire Hotel, April 19, 1994.

Landers, Elizabeth. "Trumpet: I will 'destroy' Johnson amendment," *CNN,* February 2, 2017 (accessed August 14, 2017 at http://1ref.us/lx).

Luther, Martin. *The Babylonian Captivity of the Church* (accessed August 14, 2017 at http://1ref.us/l4).

Luther, Martin. *The Table Talk of Martin Luther*, trans. and ed. by William Hazlett. London: H.G. Bohn, 1857.

Martin, Malachi. *The Keys of this Blood.* New York: Touchstone, 1990.

Masci, David. "The 2016 GOP field has a bumper crop of Catholic candidates," Pew Research Center, July 23, 2015 (accessed August 14, 2017 at http://1ref.us/lu).

Parish, Helen, Elaine Fulton, and Peter Webster, eds. *The Search for Authority in Reformation Europe.* Farnham: Ashgate Publishing Ltd., 2014.

Miller, Zeke, and Elizabeth Dias. "How Pope Francis Helped Broker Cuba Deal," *Time,* December 17, 2014 (accessed August 14, 2017 at http://1ref.us/lb).

Moody, Dwight L. *Men God Challenged.* Chicago, IL: Moody Publishers, 1998.

Moody, Dwight L. *Weighed and Wanting.* Chicago, IL: Revell, 1898.

Neufeld, Don F., and Julia Neuffer. *Seventh-day Adventist Bible Student's Source Book.* Washington, D.C.: Review and Herald Publishing Association, 1962.

Newman, Albert Henry. *A Manual of Church History*, vol. 1, rev. ed. Philadelphia, PA: The Judson Press, 1933.

Nichol, Francis D., ed. "Additional Note on Chapter 7," *Seventh-day Adventist Bible Commentary,* vol. 4. Washington, DC: Review and Herald Publishing Association, 1955.

Obama, Barack. "Statement by the President on Pope Francis' Encyclical," June 18, 2015 (accessed August 14, 2017 at http://1ref.us/ld).

O'Brien, John. *The Faith of Millions.* Huntington, IN: Our Sunday Visitor, Inc., 1974.

O'Collins, Gerald, Harry Lee Poe, and Jimmy H. Davis. *God and the Cosmos: Divine Activity in Space, Time and History.* Downers Grove, IL: InterVarsity Press, 2012.

Our Sunday Visitor, February 5, 1950.

Palmer, Tony. Address to evangelical leaders (accessed August 14, 2017 at http://1ref.us/km).

Plass, Edwald M., ed. *What Luther Says: An Anthology,* vol. 2. St. Louis, MO: Concordia Publishing House, 1959.

Pollen, John Hungerford. "The Counter-Reformation," *The Catholic Encyclopedia*, vol. 4. New York: Robert Appleton Company, 1908 (accessed August 14, 2017 at http://1ref.us/m0).

The Pontifical Biblical Commission. *The Jewish People and Their Sacred Scriptures in the Christian Bible*, sec. 27, 2001 (accessed August 14, 2017 at http://1ref.us/li).

Pope Benedict XVI. *Sacramentum Caritatis*: *Post-Synodal Apostolic Exhortation on the Eucharist as the Source and Summit of the Church's Life and Mission* (accessed August 14, 2017 at http://1ref.us/lo).

Pope Boniface VIII. *Unam Sanctum,* 1302 (accessed August 14, 2017 at http://1ref.us/kx).

Pope Francis. *Laudato Si,* May 24, 2015 (accessed August 14, 2017 at http://1ref.us/lc).

Pope Francis. Online video (accessed August 14, 2017 at http://1ref.us/kw).

Pope Gregory the Great. "Letter to Emperor Mauricius Augustus," in *Epistles*, bk. 7, letter 33, trans. in *Nicene and Post-Nicene Fathers*, ser. 2, vol. 12.

Pope John Paul II. *Ad Tuendam Fidem*, canon 1436, art. 1, May 18, 1998 (accessed August 14, 2017 at http://1ref.us/lm).

Pope John Paul II. *Crossing the Threshold of Hope.* New York: Alfred A. Knoff, 1995.

Pope John Paul II. *Dies Domini,* ch. 4, par. 67, May 31, 1998 (accessed August 14, 2017 at http://1ref.us/ln).

Pope Leo XIII. "On the Chief Duties of Christians as Citizens," January 10, 1890, trans. in *The Great Encyclical Letters of Pope Leo XIII.* New York: Benziger, 1903.

Pope Paul VI. *Lumen Gentium*, par. 18, November 21, 1964 (accessed August 14, 2017 at http://1ref.us/kr).

Pope Paul VI. *Populorum Progressio*, par. 78, 1967 (accessed August 14, 2017 at http://1ref.us/l9).

Presbyterian Church in the U.S.A. *The Protestant Reformation and Its Influence, 1517-1917.* BiblioLife, 2015.

"Public Sees Religion's Influence Waning." Pew Research Center, September 22, 2014 (accessed August 14, 2017 at http://1ref.us/lw).

Publications of the Catholic Truth Society, vol. 29. Catholic Truth Society: 1896.

Rupert, Bethany. "The Sunday Rest Bill and the Battle to Keep the Civil Sabbath," *Seton Hall Legislative Journal,* vol. 39:2 (accessed August 14, 2017 at http://1ref.us/lp).

"Sacrament of Penance," Catholic Online (accessed August 14, 2017 at http://1ref.us/kz).

Saint Catherine Catholic Church Sentinel, May 21, 1995. Algonac, MI.

Santayana, George. *The Life of Reason* (Charles Scribner's Sons: New York, 1905).

Santorum, Rick. Speech at College of St. Mary Magdalen, October 11, 2011 (accessed August 14, 2017 at http://1ref.us/lv)

Santorum, Rick. Interview with George Stephanopoulos (accessed August 14, 2017 at http://1ref.us/lv).

Schaff, Philip. *History of the Christian Church,* vol. 3. Edinburg: T&T Clark, 1884.

Schuller, Robert. *Calvary Contender.* November 15, 1987.

Schwab, Nikki. "Arizona Senator Suggests That Church Be Mandatory," *U.S. News & World Report,* March 27, 2015 (accessed August 14, 2017 at http://1ref.us/lz).

"Scripture and Tradition" (accessed August 14, 2017 at http://1ref.us/kt).

Shea, John Gilmary, et. al. *The Cross and the Flag, Our Church and Country.* New York: The Catholic Historical League of America, 1899.

Shea, John Gilmary. "The Observance of Sunday and Civil Laws for Its Enforcement," *The American Catholic Quarterly Review*, 8, January 1883.

Singman, Jeffrey L. *Daily Life in Medieval Europe.* Westport, CT: Greenwood Press, 1999.

Smith, Uriah. *Daniel and the Revelation.* Nashville, TN: Southern Publishing Association, 1944.

Standish, Colin, and Russell Standish. *The Lord's Day.* Rapidan, VA: Hartland Publications, 2002.

Theodosian Code 16.10.1, trans. by Clyde Pharr. Princeton, NJ: Princeton University Press, 1952.

Thomas, C.F. Chancellor of Cardinal Gibbons. Letter, November 11, 1895.

Tierney, Brian, and Peter Linehan. *Authority and Power: Studies on Medieval Law and Government Presented to Walter Ullmann on His Seventieth Birthday.* Cambridge: Cambridge University Press, 1980.

Tonias, Demetrios. "Sunday as a Mark of Christian Unity" (accessed August 14, 2017 at http://1ref.us/ll).

Triumphus, Augustinus. "De Papalis Sentencie Apellatione," *Summa de Potestate Ecclesiastica,* fol. 61 v. Augsburg: Augustae Vindelicorum, 1483.

Wangsness, Lisa. "Pope has chance to reclaim 'moral authority' in visit," *The Boston Globe,* September 23, 2015 (accessed August 14, 2017 at http://1ref.us/le).

Webster, William. "Did I Really Leave the Holy Catholic Church?" in *Roman Catholicism*, John Armstrong, ed. Chicago, IL: Moody Press, 1994.

Wesley, John. *Explanatory Notes on the New Testament.* London: W. Bowyer, 1754.

White, Ellen G. *The Great Controversy.* Boise, ID: Pacific Press Publishing Association, 1911.

White, Ellen G. *The Spirit of Prophecy*, vol. 4. Battle Creek, MI: Review and Herald Publishing Association, 1884.

Wilhelm, Joseph. "Apostolic Succession," *The Catholic Encyclopedia*, vol. 1. New York: Robert Appleton Company, 1907 (accessed August 14, 2017 at http://1ref.us/kq).

Wohlberg, Steve. *End Time Delusions.* Shippensburg, PA: Destiny Image Publishers, Inc., 2004.

TEACH Services, Inc.
PUBLISHING

CPSIA information can be obtained
at www.ICGtesting.com
Printed in the USA
FFOW03n1359260318
46079005-47026FF